James Harrison Wilson

Survey of the Illinois River

Letter from Secretary of War, communicating the report of Brevet Major

General J.H. Wilson on the survey and examination of the Illinois River

James Harrison Wilson

Survey of the Illinois River
*Letter from Secretary of War, communicating the report of Brevet Major General
J.H. Wilson on the survey and examination of the Illinois River*

ISBN/EAN: 9783337240561

Printed in Europe, USA, Canada, Australia, Japan

Cover: Foto ©ninafisch / pixelio.de

More available books at **www.hansebooks.com**

LETTER

FROM

SECRETARY OF WAR,

COMMUNICATING

The report of Brevet Major General J. H. Wilson on the survey and examination of the Illinois river.

MARCH 29, 1867.—*Resolved,* That there be printed of the report of Brevet Major General J. H. Wilson, upon the survey and examination of the Illinois river, when presented, seven hundred and fifty extra copies for the use of the House, and two hundred and fifty for the use of the Bureau of Engineers.

WAR DEPARTMENT,
Washington City, May 14, 1867.

SIR : In compliance with the resolution of the House of Representatives of March 26, 1867, the Secretary of War directs the accompanying report of Brevet Major General J. H. Wilson, on the survey and examination of the Illinois river, to be sent to the Congressional Printer.

Very respectfully, your obedient servant,

ED. SCHRIVER,
Inspector General.

The CONGRESSIONAL PRINTER, *Washington, D. C.*

ENGINEER DEPARTMENT,
Washington, May 13, 1867.

SIR : In compliance with the resolution of the House of Representatives of the 15th March last, I transmit herewith a copy of the report of Brevet Major General J. H. Wilson, on the survey of the Illinois river.

The act of June 23, 1866, authorized the survey of Illinois river from La Salle to its mouth.

This survey was placed in charge of Brevet Major General J. H. Wilson, lieutenant colonel 35th infantry, August 14, 1866.

At first he was instructed to restrict his operations to the survey of the river from its mouth to La Salle, but subsequently, to continue the examination of the Illinois river as far towards its source as there might be reason to believe it susceptible of improvement for the purposes of commerce and navigation.

General Wilson assigned Mr. S. T. Abert, civil engineer, to the immediate charge of the survey, who began his work at La Salle on the 1st of October, and finished at Grafton 28th November.

His object in the survey was to obtain such specific and accurate data as to be enabled to form estimates for the improvement of the river, so that the largest boats of the Illinois and Michigan canal, and steamboats drawing four feet of water, could pass through the river to the Mississippi during the season of extreme low water.

Having obtained access to the maps and profiles of a survey in 1858 of the Illinois river by Mr. J. B Preston, civil engineer, he was enabled, by comparing these with the result of his own examination, to make a more comprehensive report thah he could otherwise have obtained the data for in the short time intervening before winter.

The distance from the outlet of the canal at La Salle to Grafton, at the mouth of the Illinois, is 224 miles. The difference of level between the two points in the plane of low water is 29 feet.

The river varies in width from 500 feet at La Salle to nearly 1,400 feet at Six-mile island, with an occasional widening to something over a mile.

In ordinary and high-water stages it affords good navigation for the largest class of steamboats used on the Mississippi, while at low-water it can only be used by the smallest class of flat-bottomed boats.

The whole distance from the mouth of the Illinois river to Bridgeport, near Chicago, by river and canal, is about 320 miles; and the lockage between the two points (ordinary water-level of Lake Michigan and low-water of the Mississippi) is about 170 feet, which, by making a thorough cut from Chicago river to Lockport, on the Des Plaines, would be all descending lockage, with the lake as a summit.

General Wilson recommends the improvement of the Illinois river by a system of locks and dams at such points between Lockport and Grafton as may be determined upon as most advantageous after full and careful surveys, and that the navigation be extended from Lockport to Chicago, by the enlargement of part of the Illinois and Michigan canal, giving a depth of seven feet both in the river and canal, with locks 350 feet long and 75 wide. These dimensions he deems sufficient to pass the largest boats, either commercial or naval, that can navigate the Mississippi during the ordinary boating season.

Six dams and six locks are deemed sufficient for the improvement of the river below La Salle, and it is believed that their final location would not be far from the following points—beginning at the mouth of the river and ascending :

Lock No. 1, and dam, at Six-mile island, (probable cost)......	$491, 149
Lock No. 2, and dam, at Columbia, (probable cost)..........	459, 746
Lock No. 3, and the Naples dam, (probable cost).....	405, 746
Lock No. 4, and dam, at Frederick, (probable cost)...... ....·.	420, 746
Lock No. 5, and dam, at Spring lake, (probable cost).........	394, 622
Lock No. 6, and dam, at Chillicothe, (probable cost)..........	415, 688
Total...	2, 587, 697
Add for dredging, damage to lands, and contingencies........	536, 099
Whole cost.......................................	3, 123, 796

The distance from La Salle to Chicago is 97 miles. It is proposed to cut down the present summit to low-water level of the lake. With the exception of short canals between Lockport and Joliet, and at the Marseilles rapids it is deemed advisable to abandon the old location and to improve the natural chan-

nel of the river by locks and dams, they being less expensive than the enlargement of the original canal.

Cost of canal from Bridgeport (4½ miles from Chicago) to Lockport, 29 miles
long, 160 feet wide, and seven feet deep, $10,098,000.

Cost of improvement from Lockport to La Salle, $8,118,200.

And the entire cost of the Illinois river improvement, including the water
communication to Lake Michigan, $21,339,996, being about $68,000 per mile.

But General Wilson believes that a careful resurvey of the whole line, and especially of the country between Chicago and La Salle, would result in a very
material reduction of the estimates.

General Wilson submits with his report a profile map, and the report of his
assistant, Mr. S. T. Abert, civil engineer.

Very respectfully, your obedient servant,

A. A. HUMPHREYS,
Brig. Gen. and Chief of Engineers, Maj. Gen. Vols.

Hon. E. M. STANTON, *Secretary of War.*

REPORT OF BREVET MAJOR GENERAL J. H. WILSON, UNITED STATES
ARMY, LIEUTENANT COLONEL THIRTY-FIFTH INFANTRY, ON THE SUR-
VEY OF THE ILLINOIS RIVER FROM LA SALLE TO ITS MOUTH.

UNITED STATES ENGINEER'S OFFICE,
DES MOINES AND ROCK ISLAND RAPIDS IMPROVEMENT
AND ILLINOIS AND ROCK RIVER SURVEYS,
Davenport, Iowa, February 15, 1867.

GENERAL: Having been charged by instructions from the Engineer department with "the survey of the Illinois river from La Salle to its mouth," provided for by act of Congress, June 23, 1866, I have the honor to submit the
following report:

The act just specified simply provides for the survey as designated above,
and gives no indication whatever of the object of the survey, or the kind of
improvement which it is intended to illustrate. It was assumed, however, that,
as the general government had originally provided for the improvement of the
Illinois river by dredging its bars to a navigable depth, and had actually expended
a considerable sum of money in operations of this sort, this act in question specially requires estimates for the completion of this plan. Under date of September 13, 1866, I received the following from the Engineer department: " Minute
instructions have not been given to you in relation to these surveys, since the
intentions of Congress were not fully known to the department. Especially is
this the case with the survey of the Illinois river, as no report from this department to Congress was made during the last session when the appropriation was
made. The supposition is that the survey of this river has immediately in view
its capacity for navigation to La Salle for the largest possible class of steamers
that the river will admit when certain obstructions shall have been removed,
and ultimately the determination of canal facilities with Lake Michigan, and
the solution of the question of an adequate supply of water from Lake Michigan
as a reservoir for the canal and river during periods of low water. The act of
appropriation, however, only provides for the survey of the river from its mouth
to La Salle, and to this your operations must be restricted."

Subsequently, by letter from the Engineer department, dated January 8, 1867,
I was directed to continue the examination of the Illinois river as far towards its
source as there may be reason to believe that it is susceptible of improvement
for the purposes of commerce and navigation.

In doing this I was specially directed not to delay the preparation of such preliminary reports as might have been already begun. In reply to this letter I informed the chief engineer, January 12, 1867, that owing to the inclemency of the season it would be impossible to resume operations in the field, and that the funds applicable to the survey would not more than defray the expenses of working up the information already obtained.

Under the original instructions of the Engineer bureau relating to the survey of the Rock river, and dated August 4, 1866, I was charged particularly with the consideration and study of the subject of steamboat communication between the Mississippi and northern lakes.

As this is a matter of vast importance to the national defence, as well as to the agricultural and commercial interests of a large and productive portion of the country, I have taken the liberty of giving my investigations the widest scope consistent with the objects in view, the limited amount of funds appropriated, and the short time which could be devoted to the work. I have conferred freely with Governor Oglesby, of Illinois, whom I have to thank for his liberality and promptitude in securing information beyond my reach ; with Mr. Gooding, secretary of the Illinois and Michigan Canal Company, an engineer of enlarged experience, and have consulted every other accessible source of information, either in Illinois, Wisconsin, or the archives of the Engineer bureau. The information thus obtained, together with that derived from the survey and examination made under my directions, is embodied herein, and is believed to be sufficiently explicit to give a general understanding of the entire subject under consideration, and to enable us to determine definitely the kind of improvement which can be most effectively and advantageously applied.

In order to carry out the instructions of the bureau of engineers heretofore cited, I assigned my assistant, Mr. S. T. Abert, civil engineer, to the immediate charge of the survey of the Illinois river, aided by Mr. McMath and Mr. Froben, with a party of ten or twelve subordinates. He began the survey at La Salle on the 1st of October, and finished it at Grafton on the 28th of November, although he was considerably delayed, both in the beginning and progress of the work, by defective instruments. After some forty or fifty miles had been made, October 15, I directed Mr. Guy Wells, civil engineer, to report to Mr. Abert, and authorized the employment of such additional axemen, rodmen, and boatmen as might be necessary to complete the work before the beginning of winter. On the 16th of September I gave Mr. Abert the following instructions :

" The object of this survey is to obtain such specific and accurate information in regard to the obstructions to navigation in that river as will enable you to submit estimates for its improvement, so that the largest boats navigating the Illinois and Michigan canal, and steam boats drawing four feet of water, will be enabled to pass through the river to St. Louis during the season of extreme low water without breaking cargo. To this end you will examine and carefully delineate the various features of the river at and in the vicinity of the difficult bars and shoals ; projecting your maps of these localities on a scale sufficiently large to show the amount of excavation necessary in order that the water may be sufficiently deepened. You will observe, as far as may be practicable, the specific cause of the bars and shoals ; the influence of islands and bends of the river ; the width, depth, velocity, and cross-section, with capacity of the back-channels or chutes at the islands, and of the river itself at the *locality* of the obstructions; the width of the bottom lands ; and, in general, will obtain every class of information likely to throw light upon the entire subject of improvement, whether by dredging, wing-dams, or other means.

" The river having been already surveyed several times it may not be necessary to accurately triangulate it through its entire length, although it is desirable to have its fall from the initial point of the survey to its mouth accurately determined.

"For the rapid and economical prosecution of your work you are authorized to divide it into two or three sections, with a 'sub-party' in each; but you will keep constantly in view the fact that the means at our disposal, though limited, must be made to accomplish the important purposes of the survey."

Soon after this I learned that a complete survey of the Illinois river had been made in 1858 by Mr. J. B. Preston, civil engineer, and that the maps and profiles were on file at Lockport, Illinois. I proceeded to that place with Mr. Abert, and through the courtesy of Mr. William Gooding, secretary of the Illinois and Michigan Canal Company, I was permitted to examine them, when it occurred to me that, if they could be obtained and verified, we should be able to make a much more comprehensive report than we could possibly do by confining ourselves to such information as could be developed by our own survey between that time and winter.

At my suggestion Mr. Preston's maps, profiles, and notes were bought by Governor Oglesby for the State of Illinois and placed at my command.

In consideration of this valuable information, and the national interests involved in the improvement of the Illinois river, I became convinced that no system would be entirely effective which did not look to the extension of good navigation for the largest class of river steamers from the mouth of the river to Chicago, on the lake.

I therefore directed Mr. Abert to verify the results of Mr. Preston's survey, and to make his own "complete at every cost," or as nearly so as the high water and the lateness of the season would permit.

By an examination of his report, herewith submitted, it will be seen that the distance from the outlet of the canal at La Salle, the initial point of the survey, to Grafton, at the mouth of the Illinois river, is 224 miles; the difference of level between these two points in the plane of low water is 29.6 feet. The river varies in width from 500 feet at La Salle to nearly 1,400 feet at Six-mile island, with an occasional widening to something over a mile. In ordinary and high stages of water it affords good navigation for the largest class of steamboats used on the Mississippi river, while at the low water or dry season it cannot be used at all, except by the smallest class of flat-bottomed boats capable of carrying scarcely any cargo whatever.

The distance from the mouth of the Illinois river to Bridgeport near Chicago by river and canal is about 320 miles, and the lockage between the two points (the ordinary water level of the lake, and low water of the Mississippi river) is, as nearly as may be, 170 feet—all of which will become descending lockage, with the lake as a summit, by making a through cut from the Chicago river to Lockport on the Des Plaines. In this respect the improvement will be almost unique, and will possess an advantage in its inexhaustible summit, which will make it superior to any other artificial navigation of like extent ever constructed.

By reference to the profile of the Illinois and Michigan canal, it is found that the highest point of the dividing ridge between the Des Plaines river and the Chicago river or harbor is fourteen feet above the surface of the water in the latter, and that the natural banks of the canal are on an average ten feet above the same level for three and three-quarter miles, nine feet for eleven and one-quarter miles, and about five feet for the remaining distance. This would give a cut averaging in depth from twelve to twenty-one feet for a canal carrying seven feet water from Lake Michigan to the Des Plaines, which, with the Kankakee, forms the Illinois river. It is ascertained, quite certainly, that of this material 10,500,000 cubic yards are earth, 500,000 cubic yards hard rock, and 2,000,000 soft rock, in order to give a canal 160 feet in width, leading from the harbor of Chicago at Bridgeport to the Des Plaines at Lockport. From the latter point to La Salle, the river, with the exception of about thirty-six miles in all, can be improved by locks and dams, at a comparatively light expense in

time and money, and give thus a connected and homogeneous system of navigation from Lake Michigan to the Mississippi river.

With this statement of facts, the main difficulties to be encountered in the
construction of this system of water communication will be sufficiently understood, while the feasibility of the work, together with the principal arguments
in its favor, are strongly suggested.

The necessity for cheap water communication between the food-producing
States of the west and the Atlantic cities has been too much discussed within
the last year to require attention in this part of my report. I advert to it here
for the purpose of calling to mind one powerful and controlling reason for the
adoption of such a plan of improvement on the Illinois river as will extend its
benefits to the utmost possible limits.

In accordance with the instructions of the bureau, I have caused Mr. Abert
to prepare a careful estimate of the cost of dredging this river to a navigable
depth of four feet. By reference to his report, it will be seen that ten dredge-
boats of fifteen-horse power, working three seasons, at an aggregate cost of
$1,528,450, will be required to do the necessary dredging This is a liberal
calculation, but owing to the small quantity of water in the river at the dry
season, its shallowness on the bars, and the large amount of excavation, it is
believed that the work cannot be done with satisfactory results for a less sum
or in a shorter time.

This plan of improvement, although it applies to a part of the river only, and
cannot be depended upon to give more than four feet navigation under the most
favorable circumstances, without a feeder from the lake, has many friends along
the river. This is due, however, in many cases to the belief that any other
plan will unfavorably affect the interests of some towns and localities, and un-
duly benefit others. But such considerations as these, whether well or ill-
founded, are not of sufficient importance to exert a material influence in the
solution of the questions under discussion. There is no doubt that dredging
alone, or, at most, dredging and a feeder from the lake, can be made to answer
every purpose in the improvement of the Illinois river, if it is to be considered
as independent navigation of no other than local importance; but it must be remembered that this river is not the exclusive property of those living upon its
banks. It forms already an important link in a network of river navigation extending, with its various branches, through seventeen States of the Union, and
is destined at no distant day to become the great commercial highway between
the productive States of the west and northwest and the markets of the world.

The Illinois river seems to have been specially designed by nature as the
line by which the waters of Lake Michigan are to be connected with those of the
Mississippi. Its two principal tributaries, the Des Plaines and the Kankakee,
rising the one in Wisconsin and the other in Indiana, run for many miles
almost parallel with the western and southern lake shore, and are separated
from the lake basin by a ridge of insignificant height and width. A moment's
consideration will show that at no remote period the waters of the lake must
have been carried off by these streams as well as by the St Lawrence. It has
been already shown that the highest point of this ridge on the line of the Illinois and Michigan canal is only 14 feet above the ordinary level of the water
in the Chicago river at Bridgeport, and it is by no means certain that a lower
line may not be found by a careful survey. In fact, it is the opinion of many
old contractors who are well acquainted with the entire region, that a much
more favorable location for a steamboat canal can be obtained from Bridgeport
to section 46 of the present canal, by following the line through Mud lake,
But let this result be as it may, the data herein contained, together with the
existence of a canal of limited capacity already in operation, demonstrate
beyond a doubt that the waters of the lake may be carried into the Illinois
river through a navigable channel of any required dimensions, and at a cost

which cannot be regarded as excessive when the objects to be obtained are duly considered.

As all the lockage will be descending from the lake, it is apparent that the only limit to the capacity of the canal will be that which depends upon the velocity with which the locks can be filled and emptied. The summit will be inexhaustible, and this cannot be said of any other practicable line of water communication between Lake Michigan and the Mississippi.

In my report on the survey of the Rock river, and its connections with Green bay, it will be shown that while that line will afford ample facilities for a commercial canal having locks 200 feet long, 30 feet wide, and 7 feet deep, it will be impossible to go beyond these limits on account of the lack of water in Lake Horicor, the summit, from which the canal will descend both ways. It is believed that similar difficulties would be experienced on the line of the Fox and Wisconsin rivers. As the aggregate lockage on the former line is 617 feet, on the latter 327 feet at least, and on the Illinois river line only 170 feet, with Lake Michigan for a summit, there is no possible room to doubt which of these routes presents the greatest advantages for the construction of a steamboat canal.

From the foregoing considerations, I have the honor to recommend the improvement of the Illinois river by a system of locks and dams, to be placed at such points between Lockport and Grafton as may be determined, after a full and careful survey, to be the most advantageous; and that navigation shall be extended to the harbor of Chicago by the enlargement of the Illinois and Michigan canal, so as to adapt it to the use of the largest boats plying upon the Mississippi river. This will require a depth of 7 feet both in the canal and river, and the locks to be 350 feet long between the mitre-sills, by 75 feet wide. These dimensions are sufficient to pass the largest boat, either of commercial or naval character, that can navigate the Mississippi during the ordinary boating season, and can be made to pass naval vessels of even greater draught than seven feet by using camels or barges for lifting them partially out of the water.

It is not thought necessary to calculate for a depth sufficient to accommodate the largest lake boats, since it would require at least fourteen feet of water, and could never be used, owing to the fact that that depth could not be obtained in the Illinois and Mississippi, except during seasons of freshets.

Beside, for commercial purposes, the lake boats would be unwieldy and unprofitable on the rivers, while the river boats could not be trusted at all upon the lakes. In other words, the produce of the west, on its way to eastern markets, must be transferred to a different class of vessels as soon as it reaches the lakes; and hence, in determining the dimensions of the canal, it will be amply sufficient for all practicable purposes to arrange it for the navigation of the largest class of river steamboats. It will be remembered that the western steamboats are built with over-hanging guards, so that about 75 feet wide over all will not usually exceed 45 feet in the hull. Assuming this as a maximum width of hull, with a depth of six and a half feet, the theoretical width of the water surface in which the boat could move as in an indefinite expanse would be 202 feet, and the cross section 1,898 square feet. It is thought, however, by engineers of experience, that a width of 160 feet and a depth of seven feet will be sufficient for all practicable purposes; hence the estimates herewith submitted are based upon the latter dimensions.

It is not intended in this report to accurately fix the dimensions of the canal, nor to definitely determine the number of dams which may be required in the river improvement. It is evident that the amount of water which may be brought by the canal, as a feeder, to the river, will, in some degree, ameliorate the low-water condition of the latter. It may, therefore, materially affect the question of river improvement, and modify, in some degree, the dimensions which should be given to the canal itself. Neither the exact measure of this influence upon the river, nor the best dimensions for the canal as a feeder, can be determined till the Illinois river is more accurately surveyed during the low-water season.

We can assert confidently, however, that the interests of commerce and the national defence require navigation between Lake Michigan and the Mississippi river for the largest river steamboats; that all the physical circumstances unite in making the line, by the way of the Illinois and Michigan canal and Illinois river, as the only feasible route for such a work, and that, therefore, the enlargement of the canal, and the improvement of the river by locks and dams as herein described, are demanded by considerations of economy as well as by the public welfare.

The cost of this system of improvements, from the best information which can be obtained at present, is estimated at $21,373,906; but it is believed that a careful, resurvey of the whole line, under the auspices of the general government, in addition to obtaining much valuable and necessary information, will result in the reduction of the estimate just given several millions of dollars. As a preliminary to the commencement of the work, however, a detailed and careful survey should be made of the country between the Chicago river and La Salle, and particularly of the Illinois river, from the latter place to Lockport, with the view of determining the cost and best location for the improvement on that part of the line. It is quite evident, from what is already known, that steamboat navigation can be more cheaply provided between Lockport and La Salle by following the line of the river than by enlarging the canal; a fair estimate of the probable difference of cost has already been arrived at, and will be given hereafter; but more reliable and satisfactory calculations can be based upon a new survey made under government auspices.

In order to arrive accurately at the condition and character of the Illinois river throughout its entire length during the dry season, and to ascertain the quantity of water which flows through it under the most unfavorable circumstances as they now exist, and the quantity, if any, which it will be necessary to bring from the lake for the purposes of navigation during the low-water season, a careful hydrographic survey must be made during the most favorable summer months. The sum of $20,000 will be required for this and the survey between Chicago and La Salle. I have the honor, therefore, to recommend the immediate appropriation of that amount, so that the work may be begun as soon as practicable.

This appropriation might also be made to cover an examination of the country between the Illinois and Rock rivers, with the view of ascertaining the most feasible line for connecting the two streams by a navigable canal. The latter project has already engaged the serious attention of the counties locally interested, on account of the very great advantages which it would give to them, as well as the people of the Upper Mississippi, in the choice of markets for their surplus products. Should the Rock river ever be developed, either by the government or by private enterprise, into a great commercial line of communication, and I entertain no doubt that this will be necessary at no remote period, the connecting link between it and the Illinois river will become scarcely less important than either of the main lines.

The State of Illinois has taken this matter in hand, and during its recent session of its legislature has passed a law providing ultimately for the improvements recommended herein, and as a preliminary measure has authorized the immediate construction of a dam and lock between La Salle and Peoria. This work will be under the charge of Illinois commissioners, but should not be definitely located and begun till its relations with the entire system of improvements have been accurately determined by a board of competent engineers.

From the foregoing statement it will be seen that I favor an improvement of the Illinois river, and the construction of a canal, amply capable of carrying the lakes the largest boats which navigate the Mississippi river, and I desire to state that I recommend improvements of such magnitude after the fullest consideration of the subject, believing that nothing else will answer the present and future demands of the national defence, and sufficiently provide for the immense internal commerce of the country.

A thorough discussion of these improvements in their military, commercial, and political aspects, even if necessary, would be out of place at this time, but I cannot forego a passing allusion to them. The recent confederation of the British American provinces shows the anxiety felt by the English government in this behalf, and must be regarded as a movement in hostility to the people and institutions of the United States. While it does not actually increase the aggregate British strength on our nothern frontier, nor in any way encroach upon our territorial rights, it consolidates the policy in regard to canals,* as well as other matters, and renders available the entire force of those provinces in any difficulty which may arise between England and the United States. The English are already able, by means of a system of internal canals, to pass gunboats of nine feet draught into Lakes Erie and Ontario, and are contemplating a new canal which will enable them to reach Huron without coming in reach of American territory at any point. The canals already finished were constructed avowedly for military as well as commercial purposes, and in case of war will enable the English to drive our commerce from the lakes and destroy or lay under contribution nearly every important city on our northern frontier. But in addition they can inflict upon us a still more vital injury when they have gotten possession of the lakes by severing the *main line of our communication with the east for heavy products.*

Now that the act of confederation has become a law, the Canadians themselves will be able, and in fact compelled, to adopt a fixed policy in reference to the extension of their internal canal system, as much for offence in the possible contingency of a war with us, as for the purpose of establishing close and safe communication with the remoter portions of their territory bordering upon the upper lakes. In view of what the provinces have done in their separate capacity, it is fair to assume that they will not be neglectful of their opportunities as a united nation, but will, at the earliest possible date, set earnestly to work to enlarge, extend, and perfect their means of reaching the internal seas upon our northern borders.

We are debarred by treaty stipulations from keeping a navy upon the lakes, and this may be well enough since it saves us the expense of building costly vessels and maintaining them in commission when they are not actually required. But as we have no communication between the lakes and the seacoast suitable for vessels of war, we cannot expect to meet the enemy upon anything like terms of equality when the emergency arises. It will not do to depend upon permanent defences for the purpose of barring the entrance to the lakes, for unfortunately they cannot be so situated, nor so constructed, as to completely subserve the object in view.

There are but two ways in which we can thoroughly protect our northern frontier in times of war, and relieve ourselves of a continuous menace in times of peace. The government must either *connect the lakes and the Mississippi river by a canal of sufficient capacity to accommodate gunboats suitable for service on the lakes, or prepare for the annexation or conquest of Canada.* As a military measure the construction of a canal will be effective, and fortunately for the country this can be done at an expense which must be regarded as insignificant when compared with the objects to be obtained. But great as are the military reasons which favor the establishment of steamboat navigation between the lakes and the Mississippi, they are vastly transcended by those of a commercial and political character. The lakes, St. Lawrence river, and the New York canals are the natural outlet for the lake cities and a great portion of our northwestern territory as much as the Mississippi river is the outlet for the territory contiguous to it. Since the construction of the St. Lawrence and New York canals the commerce of the northwestern and western States has gradually been seeking its way to the eastern seaboard rather than to the southern. Indeed, the northern tier of our States, even as far west as the Missouri, owe their prosperity, if not their existence, to the development of water communication with the east. Railroads have exerted a potent influence in populating these States, but their extraordinary development in wealth and industry is mainly due to the construction of the Canadian and New York canals, by which, up to the present time, they have been able to send their surplus products directly and cheaply to market. This fact accounts satisfactorily for the superior wealth of the country bordering directly upon the lakes, and for the marvellous growth of the cities which have sprung into existence along our northern borders within the last forty years.

But owing to various restrictions, and to the influence of certain commercial laws, it has been found unprofitable and inconvenient of late to use the St. Lawrence canals, while the New York canals are already overtaxed, and the region west of Chicago is almost entirely unprovided with canal facilities worthy of the name. So that a great part of the people of Illinois, Iowa, Wisconsin, Minnesota, and Missouri, are compelled to send their surplus products to market by rail or perilous river navigation, at an expense in money or time which leaves them scarcely a tithe of their value to pay for the cost of production.

These States have now reached a stage in their development when cheap and direct communication with the markets of the world has become an absolute commercial necessity, and unless the amplest provision is made by our own government for such communication, and a policy adopted by Canada which shall give us all the advantages of unrestricted trade upon their rivers and canals, our commerce and agriculture will be crippled before the expiration of another decade, to such an extent as to demand not only the enlargement of the Illinois and Michigan canal, the improvement of the Illinois river, and the construction of the Rock River and Green Bay canal, but the absolute conquest or annexation of the entire Canadian confederation.

To the people of our race nothing is more inexorable than a commercial necessity, no argument is so potent as that based upon physical facts, and no ethics so readily understood as those which relate to the national welfare. When our people have been brought to thoroughly understand this necessity, the facts which underlie it, and the manner in which it affects their material well-being, they will not be over-nice in regard to the territorial rights of those who bar the door to the eastern market, but will demand the extension of our borders so that their commerce may find its way "unvexed to the sea" by the St. Lawrence, as it now does by the Mississippi.

One of our ablest writers and thinkers, in " Thoughts upon the civil policy of America," has given it as his opinion that " it should be a settled principle of American legislation to encourage in every possible way facilities for intercommunication, to repress in the most effectual way anything that might possibly act as a restraint." And adds, that " experience shows that travel increases as its cost diminishes." Whatever, therefore, operates as a tax on locomotion is inconsistent with the highest principles of state policy. No community should be permitted to take advantage of the geographical position it may happen to occupy for the purpose of exacting a toll for its own profit. Such practices may suit an Arab sheikh, or other Asiatic chieftain, who levies a contribution on the passing caravan, but it is altogether inadmissible in a modernized society. A community cannot perpetrate this act without becoming politically debauched and demoralized. It is an offence against the highest public interests.

When the railway system was first being developed in England, measures were taken to give to the government an effectual and thorough control over it. Already in that country it is agitated to consummate those measures by the state assuming the proprietorship of the roads, equalizing their rates of charge, and reducing those rates to a minimum. There can be no doubt that such a consummation would produce very powerful social effects. In its direction it would act in the same manner that the changes in the postal system have done, those social effects being all of an advantageous kind. But England, her comparatively restricted geographical extent being considered, is not pressed by those climate considerations that are of such paramount importance in America. Her reasons for action in the matter are therefore, it may be said, of a very subordinate kind, compared with those that concern us. *In America, transportation at the lowest possible cost assumes the attitude of an affair of the highest state necessity.*"

There are but few persons of intelligence who will deny these general propositions, and if they are true in regard to social " intercommunication," who can doubt their significance when applied to the question of commercial intercommunication ? Our people are great travellers, mostly because their business requires it. By increasing the facilities for the transportation of manufactured goods and the staple products, we must inevitably increase the necessity for rapid communication between all sections. By constructing canals and improving river navigation we necessarily increase the demand for railroads.

It is related of Talleyrand that, when speaking to the Emperor Napoleon of the United States, he used these words : " It is a great giant without bones." That was before the day of railroads and canals. We have since penetrated every section of the country by railroads in abundance, " which are bones of iron;" but in our eagerness for improvement let us not forget to construct canals, which may more truthfully be called " the arteries" of our giant, and without which his life-blood must stagnate about his heart, instead of flowing to his distant extremities, vitalizing and strengthening his whole body.

There is a lesson in this which we should not fail to learn and apply to the case under consideration, for it concerns not only the national defence but our agricultural, commercial, and political welfare.

In closing this report, I beg leave to invite the attention of the Engineer department to the interesting report of my assistant, Mr. S. T. Abert, and a statement (marked Appendix A) compiled by Colonel H. A. Ulffers, civil engineer, assistant, giving an outline of the Canadian and New York canal systems, together with other interesting facts and statistics bearing upon the necessity for cheap and commodious water communication between the Mississippi river and the eastern seaboard by the way of the great lakes and their natural outlet.

I am, sir, very respectfully, your obedient servant,

J. H. WILSON,
Lieut. Col. 35th Infantry, Brevet Maj. Gen. U. S. A.
Brevet Major General A. A. HUMPHREYS,
Chief Engineer U. S. Army, Washington, D. C.

DAVENPORT, IOWA, *February* 15, 1867.

GENERAL: In obedience to your instructions, I have the honor to submit the following report, with a profile map and estimates for improving the Illinois river from La Salle (the termination of the Illinois and Michigan canal) to its entrance into the Mississippi.

Commencing at the mitre-sill of the lower lock at La Salle on the 1st day of October, 1866, the field operations terminated at Grafton, below the mouth of the river, on the 28th of November, 1866. The completion of so important an examination of a distance of two hundred and twenty-four miles, within the period above designated, was necessary, on account of the small appropriation for that object and the desire expressed in your instructions to lay information before Congress during the early part of the approaching session. Attention was strictly confined to the determination of such facts as might serve as a basis for plans and estimates for improving the river; the application of hydro-dynamic formulæ being necessarily limited by the short period allotted to that purpose.

The subject matter has been brought together under the following heads :

I. Physical features of the river and valley.

II. Method of improvement by dredging.

III. Lake Michigan as a reservoir.

IV. Improvement by locks and dams.

V. The " Illinois and Michigan" enlargement.

VI. A tabular statement of the cost of canals, and some statistical facts, are added.

I. To determine the propriety of any system of improvement, an accurate conception of the physical features of the river is requisite. The following general description may not be out of place. " If we could ship from the sur-face of the State," says Professor Worthen, " the superficial deposit of sand, clay, and gravel, we should find it intersected by broad and deep valleys cut in the solid rock. These valleys were excavated in part by streams of water, enlarged by the action of ice during the period of submergence." Other geolo-gical agencies are plainly traceable. The upheaval to which the river system of this continent is due has had a marked influence upon the course of the Illinois. Two primary axes of disturbance have determined the geographical features of this country ; one elevating the Rocky mountain range and prolonged in the Cordilleras of Mexico and South America, the other upheaving the great Appalachian chain. The waves of disturbance, diminishing from the two primary axes, subside into the synclinal line through which the Mississippi flows to the gulf of Mexico. Down one of the inclines the Illinois finds its way. In its course, two marked disturbances may be observed, one at La Salle, the other crossing the river at its mouth. At both points the river is diverted from its direct course.

In the upper part of the river the rounded form of the bluffs and the gentle slope of the secondary terrace give evidence of the action of a moderate current succeeding the glacial movement which deposited the drift and alluvion. With an average width of seven hundred feet, the Illinois, in this part of its course, flows in a depression fifty or sixty feet below the level of the bluffs. The drainage of the adjacent country is inadequate to fill the valley, which has an average width of a mile and a half. It has been inferred that the body of water which produced these rounded forms and gentle slopes found its way from Lake Michigan to the river, and that at an early day the northern lakes were alike tributaries of the gulf of St. Lawrence and the gulf of Mexico.

Through two such valleys, exhibiting similar physical characteristics, the Kankakee and Des Plaines rivers, embracing the lower extremity of Lake Michigan, unite to form the Illinois.

The geological character of the river has a practical importance in relation to works of improvement. Lower magnesian limestone, found at Utica, affords hydraulic lime of excellent quality. The mills of Clark & Company, situated at the same place, supply at moderate rates any point along the river with cement made from this stone. Trenton limestone, affording good building stone, is found at La Salle ; the St. Peters limestone, of the same locality, yields the sand used in the glass works at that place. Here, also, coal is brought to the surface by an upheaval, and appears lower down the river in an out-crop of the same strata at Peoria; between this point and the mouth of the river, coal of a different kind, but of a superior quality, is found. Of building-stone, near Pekin, no specimens were obtained. An inferior sandstone was obtained at Lagrange.

Limestone, bearing the fossils which characterize the Keokuk group, was first observed above Florence; it no doubt occurs higher up the river. Weighing one hundred and eighty pounds to the cubic foot, but difficult to dress on account of hardness, this stone affords good material for rubble masonry or for the filling of crib-dams. Above Hardin, similar limestone bluffs approach the river; strata, bearing fossils similar to those of the Utica hydraulic limestone, were observed here, indicating the presence of a stone probably possessing the same properties.

Near the mouth of the Illinois river the bluffs of buff-colored dolomite (Trenton limestone) are largely quarried for building purposes. Nothing more striking appears in the course of the river than these bluffs, indicating a violent disruptive force, against which the two great rivers have beat for centuries. Entering the Mississippi the action of its more powerful current is plainly visible upon the face of the rocks. These facts indicate the existence at convenient points of abundant material for works of masonry.

The Illinois is supplied by drainage from a prairie country, rather exceeding in area twenty-seven thousand square miles. To the absence of mountains and hills within this area the gradual increase and slow subsidence of floods is to be attributed.

The entire length of the river, estimating either one of its tributaries as a part, is about 330 miles; the distance from La Salle, the head of unimproved navigation, to Grafton, at the mouth of the river, is 224 miles; the fall in this distance, in the plane of ordinary low water, is 29.6 feet; the fall in the high-water plane of 1858, as determined from local testimony, was 29.2 feet. The low water of the Mississippi has an important influence upon the navigable condition of the Illinois, and may prolong the duration of the low-water period and diminish the inclination of the low-water plane. I do not anticipate an increase of inclination in the same plane, as the figures given above are supposed to represent the maximum.

As the survey advanced, tide scales were placed at nearly regular intervals, and observers were employed to note the height of the water every morning and evening. These scales were adjusted by the level, in order that all the observations might be reduced to the same zero. Some of these observations have been reduced to diagrams, which establishes the fact that the greatest inclination in the surface plane of the river during the period of the survey was 37.3 feet. This occurred when the river at La Salle was increasing from the effect of rain, while it was falling at Grafton in conformity to the Mississippi.

The river, for the entire distance surveyed, is free from rapids or falls, the average fall per mile varying from $\frac{1.3}{100}$ to $\frac{1.6}{100}$ of a foot. The velocity was, as observed at Hennepin, one-half mile per hour; at Grand Pass, rather more than three-quarters of a mile per hour; below Naples it was one and one eighth mile per hour.

It will be seen from the following table that the maximum fall per mile was $\frac{4}{10}$ of a foot, and occurs at the Beardstown bar; the minimum fall is found in Lake Peoria, being $\frac{1}{100}$ of a foot.

Table showing the average fall of water per mile at the points named in the Illinois river.

Names.	Feet.	Decimals.	Names.	Feet.	Decimals.
Peru	0	2	Between head and foot of Grand island	0	3
Hennepin	0	3	Beardstown bar	0	4
Henry	0	3	Meredosia	0	1
Lacon	0	1	Frederick	0	15
Chillicothe	0	2	Naples	0	2
Lake Peoria	0	1	Apple creek	0	23
Narrows	0	1	Six-mile island	0	08
Peoria	0	3	One mile above the mouth of the river	0	17
Pekin	0	2	Minimum fall in Lake Peoria.	0	1
Havana	0	2			
Matanzas	0	2			

With a sluggish current, indicated by the foregoing table, the river wanders through a valley of swampy land, varying in width from one and a half to six miles. During the period of the survey (averaging from six to nine feet of water on the bars) the banks were low, rising in many places to an elevation of three to eight feet above the surface of the water. Intersected by lagoons and swamps, covered with a dense growth of willow, these bottoms seem impenetrable. Such is the desolate appearance of the silent swamps and lagoons, that Captain Howard Stansbury, in a report of a survey made in 1838, expresses the opinion that they must "ever remain uninhabited." This may be true, until a denser population gives sufficient value to the land to justify a reclamation by levees. Already, cultivation has begun to encroach upon the bottoms, and where the river approaches the bluffs, thriving towns and cities have sprung up. Large elm, cottonwood, and pecan trees occupy the higher part of the bottoms, while along the bluffs, oak, suitable for building purposes, can be found.

Abraded banks appear more frequently below the escarpment of modified drift at Havana. This increase of abrasion is due, in part, to a greater elevation of the banks and a greater velocity of the current.

The general course of the Illinois river is noticeably direct; the sudden bends at La Salle and Grafton have been mentioned; the straight reaches are almost invariably deep, with a muddy bottom; the shallows occur at elbows, at confluent channels, and at the mouths of creeks. These are controlled by the general laws applicable to such situations. Without stating the exact circumstances affecting each, it may be said that all shallows below elbows are made in the dead angle of the eddy, and are caused by the deflection of the current to the concave shore; the materials swept from the low grounds at high water, or brought into the river by the rain, are deposited in the neutral axes of confluent channels, or where the river loses its velocity in a broad expanse; while the sand brought down by creeks will be deposited at the point of conflict, if the streams oppose each other, or in the backward prolongation of the resultant of the two forces, if the streams approach each other in the same general direction. From the small amount of material brought down by the floods, the shoals increase but slowly.

The longest and deepest reaches occur between Henry, Lacon, Chillicothe, and Peoria, Liverpool and Havana, Moscow and Browning, the depth, for considerable distances, varying from eighteen to thirty feet. For a distance of about fifteen miles above Peoria, the river expands to seven or eight times its ordinary width. The lower part of this fine expanse of water is known as Lake Peoria. Glacial action and the erosive force of the water, acting on unequal deposits of drift, may account for these inequalities of width and depth.

The low-water condition of the river occurs generally in the months of July, August, and September. During this period the water falls as low as eighteen or twenty inches on some of the bars; the packets cease to make regular trips, and navigation is virtually suspended. Last September the river was in good navigable condition, and remained unchanged in this respect until closed by the ice. For five months in the year the navigation is suspended by ice, and during the period of from sixty to ninety days it is reduced to barges and the smallest class of tugs.

The following table exhibits the depth of water on the bars known to the pilots or mentioned in reports of former surveys; some of these have ceased to be obstructions to navigation. This result is due to dredging operations conducted under the orders of Colonel J. E. Johnston, corps of togoraphical engineers. Reports of this work appear to have been made to Colonel Johnston, by Major G. W. Long, in 1854.

These documents must contain valuable matter, indicating, by comparison with the recent survey, the changes which have taken place in portions of the river, and the effect of dredging new channels through the shoals. Before submitting the table of shoals, it may be stated generally, that bars and shoals in the upper portion of the river are formed of sand and fine gravel, the velocity of the current being insufficient to carry this material beyond the point where it enters the main stream. Coarser gravel, the detritus of rocky bluffs, is found upon the shoals near the bluffs from whence it originated. At Beardstown, Apple creek, and other points, the river bed is composed of blue clay, in which large quantities of muscle-shell are embedded. At Otwell's bar a pole can be thrust from twenty to thirty feet in sand and mud.

Depth of water, in feet and tenths, on the following named bars, reduced to the lowest ascertained low-water plane.

[The figures in the second column are copied from the report of Captain Howard Stansbury, corps of topographical engineers, made in the year 1838; those in the first column denote the depth found by this survey, in 1866. The distances are estimated from the mouth of the Illinois and Michigan canal.]

Names of bars.	Survey of 1866.		Survey of 1838.		Distance in—	
	Feet.	Tenths.	Feet.	Tenths.	Miles.	Tenths.
Spring Creek bar	2	8	2	0	4	4
Treetop bar	1	8			6	25
Head of Crab island	2	5			7	9
Negro creek	3	1	2	0	10	5
Bureau creek	3	6	2	0	14	5
Hennepin island	2	0			15	6
Hennepin flats	2	5			16	7
Sister islands	2	0	2	0	20	7
Willow bar	2	8			22	5
Sandy creek	2	5	2	0	27	5
Brother islands			2	5	30	0
Crow creek	2	2			41	25
Peoria flats	2	8			64	4
Kickapoo creek	2	8			65	5
Lick creek	2	6			68	7
Pekin	2	6			71	6
Flats above Kingston	2	0			77	0
Lancaster bar	2	1			80	7
Copperas creek	4	1			87	4
Liverpool	2	5			95	9
Spoon river	3	5			105	1
Matanzas	3	0			109	4
Grand island	3	1	2 to 2.5		111	7
Bath	3	5			114	0
Moscow, (half mile below)	3	3			116	5
Foot of Grand island	2	8			118	7
Sangamon river	3	7			127	4
Sugar creek	3	5	2 to 2.5		131	2
Beardstown	3	0	varying from 1.5, 1.8 to 2.0		136	7
Below Cluster of Islands	3	0			139	5
Moon's island	3	0			149	1
Meredosia	3	2			154	4
First island below Meredosia	3	0			156	4
Naples bar	3	0			160	0
Naples flats or Mauvaise bar	3	0	2 to 2.5		163	1
Blue River bar	3	2	2	0	167	5
One-half mile below Florence	4	3			172	1
Bedford and Bridgeport	4	4	2	5	176	1
Grand Pass	3	6	2	0	181	9
Otwell's bar	2	7	1	8	185	7
School-house bar	3	7			187	6
Apple creek	4	2	2	0	189	0
French bar	4	0	2	5	205	1

II. METHOD OF IMPROVEMENT BY DREDGING.

The small velocity of the current, the slow increase and subsidence of floods, the comparatively small amount of sedimentary matter brought down by the river during the prevalence of high water, are circumstances favorable to improving the navigation by dredging. This method of improvement, by which a moderate expenditure is followed by immediate local results, has many friends. But small benefit is conferred by such works unless executed with a view to attain a uniform depth throughout the entire length of the river, sufficient to admit the passage of the class of steamers engaged in the ordinary river trade.

In 1854 (as near as can be ascertained) a sum of money was appropriated for the purpose of improving the river by dredging a channel of about four feet in depth throughout the bars. The survey was made, and the dredging was executed, under the instructions of Colonel J. E. Johnston, by Major G. W. Long. I have not been able to obtain a statement of the amount of work done. The tabular statement (page 16) indicates an improvement in depth at many places. The want of more full and accurate information impairs the value of conclusions drawn from this table. It is certain that the work executed at Apple creek and at other points having a clay bottom have remained without perceptible change, while that done at Treetop bar and below Hennepin, in sandy material, has been totally obliterated. In the absence of exact information as to the amount of work done, the causes of this result can be only indicated.

The upper portion of the river is reduced to a stream discharging 633 cubic feet per second at low water, giving about twenty inches on Treetop bar. Small tugs, in boring their way through sand shoals, obliterate the channels and reduce the surface to a level.

The deterioration is, also, more rapid on account of the smaller discharge and velocity of this portion of the stream. The lower portion receives tributaries navigable at high water by barges. Lagoons, giving to the river at low water the surplus stored in them during the high-water period, unite to form a larger body of water. Increase of shoals is, therefore, not so apparent in the lower part of the river. Deteriorations resulting from natural causes, operating through long periods of time, are not here enumerated. All systems of improvement are alike subject to them. This deterioration can be met by periodical expenditures.

During the past year navigation has been unusually favorable. The lowest water occurred in the months of June and November. In the first named month the depth was not less than three and a half feet, rising to nine feet in September, and falling to four feet in November.

Sufficient data is not, at present, available for determining accurately the duration of the low-water period. General F. P. Blair, in a report to Congress, recommending the improvement of the Illinois river, gives the following statement of the depths of water on the bars in 1860 : "In the month of March the depth was six feet five inches ; in April, three feet five inches ; in May, two feet and seven inches ; in August, two feet ; in September, one foot and eight inches ; in October, one foot and eight inches ; in November, two feet and five inches."

It is inferred from these facts, that while dredging as a method of improvement may be applied remediably in the lower section of the river, it cannot be applied with the same success in the upper portion without the aid of longitudinal dikes, or "wing-dams," and that these structures will prove an obstruction to navigation in the ordinary stages of the river.

The use of "wing-dams," subsidiary to dredging, either to give increased velocity at certain points by contracting the channel, or for the purpose of retarding the water which may be withdrawn from the upper reaches by new and deeper channels through the shoals, may be applied with advantage in the broader parts of the stream. Such cases belong to a class of problems best solved in the practical operation of dredging. The same remark may be extended to the expediency of uniting certain islands with the main shore, or linking them together. For this purpose no additional estimate is necessary. The material taken from the bottom may be placed in the channel it is desired to close, but in all cases it is important that the material removed from the bed of the river should be placed where it cannot be again washed into the main stream. It is an objection to this method of improvement that an excavation of a channel through the shoals will develop other shoals above the points of excavation. An uncertain amount of work may therefore be expected.

Dredging, as a method of improvement, has been applied in all the navigable rivers and harbors of the United States. The most successful operations have been conducted on the Hudson, Lake Champlain, Chesapeake bay, and the mouth of the Mississippi. A remarkably successful application of this method has been made on the river Clyde by English engineers. Where formerly but three and a half feet of water was found, vessels can now carry eighteen feet up to the city of Glasgow. This depth is maintained by dredging 180,000 tons annually.

This method of improvement, with the aid of a dam or a feeder drawing a supply of water from Lake Michigan, may be applied with advantage between La Salle and the mouth of the river; but without either of these aids it cannot be recommended for the upper section of the Illinois.

The subjoined estimate is based on the proposed excavation of a channel having 150 feet in width and a depth of five feet, affording navigation for the ordinary river packets, drawing from four to four and a half feet of water. The entire quantity to be dredged has been carefully calculated for each bar, and distributed into ten sections, corresponding to the number of dredge-boats it is proposed to employ. The quantity of each section has been equalized as nearly as the proximity of the bars would permit. By comparing this statement with the profile, the exact amount of dredging to be done at any point may be ascertained.

Tabular statement of the number of cubic yards to be dredged from each bar between La Salle and the mouth of the Illinois river, in order to give five feet of depth on all the shoals.

SECTION FIRST.

Name of bar.	Cubic yards.	Cubic yards in section.
Mouth of canal, La Salle	15,399.4	
Spring creek	49,793.5	
Treetop	60,434.2	125,627.1

SECTION SECOND.

Crab Island bar	13,685.4	
Crab Island crossing	1,172.2	
Negro Creek bar	22,927.8	
Mouth of Negro Creek bar	2,225.0	
Bureau creek	6,486.0	
Hennepin island	32,066.6	
Hennepin flats	34,669.4	113,232.4

SECTION THIRD.

Below Two Sisters	19,383.3	
Lower crossing	4,733.0	
Willow bar	23,625.0	
Henry bar	12,008.3	
Brother islands	13,800.0	
Below Chillicothe island	37,600.0	
Crow creek	9,697.0	
Peoria flats	24,794.4	
Peoria flats, continued	12,472.2	158,118.2

SECTION FOURTH.

Name of bar.	Cubic yards.	Cubic yards in section.
Kickapoo bar	24,699.1	
Below Kickapoo bar	5,358.3	
Station 600 to station 606	21,511.1	
Pekin	8,366.6	
Above Mackinaw creek	9,153.0	
Above Kingston	41,958.3	
Kingston bar	6,505.5	117,551.9

SECTION FIFTH.

Kingston bar, continued	70,959.2	
Below Kingston	15,616.6	
Lancaster bar	36,703.7	123,279.5

SECTION SIXTH.

Lancaster flats	65,323.1	
Above Canton landing	25,819.4	
Copperas creek	8,007.4	
Below Copperas creek	5,683.3	
Station 872 to station 875	8,722.2	113,555.4

SECTION SEVENTH.

Spoon River bar	6,183.3	
Spoon River bar, continued	3,613.0	
Havana	1,139.0	
Matanzas island	5,444.4	
Matanzas bar	20,012.0	
Grand Island bar	44,135.0	
Bath bar	14,824.4	
Upper Moscow	7,105.8	
Moscow bar	29,636.0	132,092.9

SECTION EIGHTH.

Foot of Grand island	22,225.0	
	2,266.6	
Sugar creek	16,328.0	
Below Frederick	4,133.3	
Above and below Beardstown	4,788.8	
Cluster of islands below Beardstown	18,928.0	
Below La Grange	18,539.0	
Moore's island	19,655.0	
Eagle island	8,605.0	115,469.7

SECTION NINTH.

Above French island	7,766.6	
Meredosia	2,266.6	
Head of second island above Naples	3,461.1	
Head of first island above Naples	6,511.1	
Naples bar	6,883.3	
Naples flats	33,563.0	
Blue river	6,316.6	
Elm island	4,005.5	
Buckhorn island	4,938.8	
Grand Pass	10,750.0	
Below Little landing	3,713.0	90,175.6

SECTION TENTH.

Name of bar.	Cubic yards.	Cubic yards in section.
Bee creek and Otwell's bar	72,976.6	
Columbiana	17,816.6	
Columbiana, continued....................................	21,516.1	
French bar..	13,055.5	
Head of Twelve-mile island	6,394.4	
	13,743.8	145,503.0

Aggregate of all the bars, 1,234,605.7 cubic yards.

The distance to which this material should be transported, and the interruption to daily operations by the frequent passage of packets and canal-boats, will prolong the time required, under favorable circumstances, to complete this work.

Three working seasons, or three years, will probably be required to complete the work, with ten dredge-boats of 15-horse power each. I have supposed Osgood's dredge will be employed, although a chain-bucket dredge might be devised to execute the work at less cost.

ESTIMATE OF THE COST OF DREDGING.

10 dredge-boats, delivered at designated points.............		$140,000 00
50 barges for transporting sand..........................		50,000 00
3 steam-tugs...		30,000 00
Cables, anchors, operating tugs..........................		30,000 00
3,600 cords of wood per year, for 10 dredges for 3 years, at $4 per cord......................................		43,200 00
Pay, rations, and lodging for 400 men for 3 working seasons..		742,900 00
For working each dredge—		
1 engineer, per day......	$5	
2 firemen, per day........	3	
1 crane tender, per day......	3	
4 anchor tenders, per day...........................	8	
1 cook, per day.....................................	2	
	—	
Total for one dredge..................	21	
For operating each dredge for one season, $3,780.		
10 dredges for three seasons............................		113,400 00
Barrows, tools, repairs, laying up......................		40,000 00
50,000 lineal feet of wing-dam, at $4 per foot.............		200,000 00
Aggregate........		1,389,500 00
Engineering and contingencies, 10 per cent...............		138,950 00
Total cost of improving the Illinois river by dredging....		1,528,450 00

III. LAKE MICHIGAN AS A RESERVOIR.

The utilization of the water of Lake Michigan as a feeder to supply the Illinois river during the low-water period; how far the number of the locks and dams, proposed to be erected for the purpose of passing the obstructions and overcoming the fall in the surface of the river, may be reduced by the supply from this source, and what may be the amount of excavation requisite to make

this method of improvement effective, and to give seven feet of water from Marseilles rapids to the Mississippi, are questions of sufficient interest and importance to merit careful consideration. Your instructions to me relating to this
subject are as follows : "The survey should have ultimately in view the solution of the question of an adequate supply of water from Lake Michigan as a
reservoir for a canal and the river during the period of low water." The close
of the season did *not allow of a special examination or survey with a view to
the complete solution of this question.* So far as relates to an adequate supply
for evaporation, lockage, and milling, an answer will be found in another part of
this report.

Certain facts and theoretical deductions are herein presented, and it is believed are sufficient to *indicate the course of examination* to be pursued in order
to solve the problem. A question of similar import has been brought conspic-
uously before the country in an ingeniously written pamphlet, prepared by the
late Colonel Charles Ellet, and published among the "Smithsonian contribu-
tions."

This gentleman proposed to preserve the navigable condition of the Ohio, by
feeding at low water from reservoirs constructed in the valleys and gorges near
the sources of that river. This plan was condemned as impracticable because
of the difficulty of constructing reservoirs of sufficient capacity. This objection
cannot apply to the plan now under consideration.

The fact that the lakes supply the impetuous torrent of the St. Lawrence, and
maintain the constant regimen of that river, strengthens the conclusion that the
comparatively small and feeble Illinois may be kept in navigable condition by
the same bountiful source. Nature has here accumulated every circumstance
favorable to the attempt. A summit of not more than ten feet separates the
lake from the river. The Des Plaines branch of the Illinois approaches to
within 12 miles of the western shore of the lake ; while the Kankakee, another
branch of the same river, may be 15 or 20 miles from the Great Calumet river, a
tributary of the lake at its lower extremity. It is evident that any desired fall
can be obtained, from the fact that the Des Plaines, at Lockport, 29 miles from
the Chicago river, and 33 miles from the lake, is 20 feet below the surface of
this great natural reservoir.

The summit level of the Illinois and Michigan canal between the last named
points is being now cut down to the standard low-water level of the lake, for
the purpose of draining the stagnant water of the Chicago river. It is estimated
that this channel will discharge 24,000 cubic feet per minute, a quantity equal
to two-thirds of the discharge of the Illinois river at Treetop bar during the low-
water stage. This supply must have an ameliorating effect upon the worst navigable condition of the river.

The quantity of water requisite to maintain the Illinois river in good navigable
condition may be reduced to calculation. Preliminary observations have been
made with a view to this object. The low-water discharge of the river at Treetop
bar, when there was 20 inches of water on that bar, as determined by an assistant
of Mr. Gooding, was 37,980 cubic feet per minute, or 633 cubic feet per second.
The discharge at Hennepin, when the river was in good condition, (*i. e.*, 7.4 feet
above low water at Hennepin, and 9 feet on Treetop bar,) was, as determined by
my observations, 311,280 cubic feet per minute, or 5,188 cubic feet per second.

To assist in determining the quantity of water to be supplied from the lake,
in order to maintain the navigable condition of the river, simultaneous observations were made upon the height of the water at different points along its course.
As these observations are important to the theoretical determination of the quantity of water to be supplied from the lake, it seems proper to be more explicit in
regard to them. The observations were made upon scales, the zeros of which
were placed to correspond with the lowest ascertained low-water plane. This
plan was established after a comparison of observations, and with the aid of the

profile of the survey of the late John B. Preston, civil engineer. The records of observations forwarded to this office give the following results :

The elevation of the river above the low-water plane (October 14) was, at La Salle, 8.4 feet; on the same day at Hennepin, it was 7.4 feet. A continuous series of observations (December 3) give elevations above zero as follows : At La Salle, 9.3 feet; Lacon, 5 4 feet; Peoria, 6 feet; Beardstown, 3.8 feet; Naples, 1.85 feet; Westport, 4.4 feet; Hardin, 2.4 feet; Grafton 2.4 feet. A discrepancy will be observed at Lacon and Naples, but may result from natural causes, as will appear from the following explanation :

A comparison of the record for seven days, when the river was rising, shows the height at Lacon approaching to an equality and gradually exceeding the reading at Peoria, and during eight subsequent days, when the river was falling, the reading of the scales at the two places resumed the same relative position it had before the rise of the water. The probable cause of this difference may be the broad expanse of the river below Lacon, terminating in Lake Peoria. The high water at Lacon, being more rapidly withdrawn into the broad space below, passes off from Lake Peoria with a slightly increased velocity, but no perceptible increase of elevation.

The parallelism in the planes of the surface water at different stages of the river, as shown by the profile, allows the interpolation of a plane of any desired height. Any deficiency in the observations may be thus supplied. Knowing therefore the depth of the water at Hennepin, and the corresponding discharge upon any given day, we are able to predict the depth of the water upon any of the bars below, if the same discharge is constantly maintained by artificial means. The accuracy of the prediction being proportionate to the care bestowed in ascertaining the low-water plane and in observing the scales.

The question to be determined is what would be the height of the surface of the river below Hennepin, at a sufficient number of points to establish its inclination during the time observations were being taken, for the purpose of estimating the discharge. The interpolated plane gives the following heights above zero : At La Salle, 8.4 feet; at Hennepin, 7.4 feet; at Lacon, 4.4 feet; at Peoria, 5 feet; at Beardstown, 2.8 feet; at Naples, 1 foot; at Westport, 3.4 feet; at Hardin, 1.4 foot, and lastly, at Grafton, 1.3 foot.

It would then appear that this stage of the river would give a navigation as follows : from La Salle to Spring lake, (below Peoria,) 7 feet; from thence to Beardstown, 5 feet; to below the Naples flats, 4 feet; thence to the mouth of the river, increasing again to 5.3 feet. If the low-water plane has been correctly ascertained and the records of the elevation of the water carefully kept, these deductions may be depended upon as sufficiently near the truth for all purposes of theory or practice. Assuming their correctness, it follows by inference that, by the aid of one, or at most two dams, together with a small amount of dredging upon some of the bars, a navigation of 6 feet depth can be obtained between La Salle and Grafton.

The next steps in the solution of the problem are : First, to determine the quantity of water to be supplied from the lake in order to maintain the depths above mentioned; and second, the dimensions of the channel and the velocity of water requisite to give the desired discharge.

The discharge at Hennepin, at a stage of water corresponding to the interpolated heights, was 5,188 cubic feet per second; the low-water discharge of the river is 633 cubic feet per second. The difference in the quantity to be supplied by the feeder is 4,555 cubic feet per second. Assuming a constant discharge equal to 4,555 cubic feet per second in channels of different widths, what will be the fall per mile and the velocity in each ?

Let the first channel be assumed as 160 feet wide; the second 200 feet wide, and the third 350 feet wide; all of them having the same depth—8 feet.

First. Channel 160 feet wide; discharge 4,555 cubic feet per second; fall per mile will be 1.11 foot; velocity 3.56 feet per second, or 2.43 miles per hour.

Second. Channel 200 feet wide; discharge 4,555 cubic feet per second; fall per mile will be 0.69 foot; velocity 2.84 feet per second, or 1.93 mile per hour.

Third. Channel 350 feet wide; discharge 4,555 cubic feet per second; fall per mile will be 0.22 foot; velocity 1.62 foot per second, or 1.104 mile per hour.*

The first channel has the same dimensions, but a greater inclination, as the proposed enlargement of the Illinois and Michigan canal. The improvement now in progress upon this line will furnish nearly two-thirds of the required discharge. May not the dimensions be so modified as to supply the entire quantity required?

The arguments in favor of the line of the present canal may be summed up as follows: First, a channel already exists requiring a small amount of alteration to adapt it to the object in view. Second, the improvement may be made accessory to the enlargement of the Chicago harbor and the drainage of that city.

A channel 160 feet wide, having a fall of 1.11 foot per mile, would give a velocity of nearly two and a half miles per hour. The resulting velocity in the Chicago river would present but little opposition to steam navigation, and can hardly be regarded as inconvenient to vessels effecting a landing at the wharves.

A channel 200 feet wide would give a velocity of nearly two miles per hour. Our information is insufficient for an estimate for the cost of this channel. The cost of modifying the proposed enlargement of the Illinois and Michigan canal so as to give the required discharge could not greatly exceed the original estimate for this enlargement.

The low-water stage of the river extending over a period of from 60 to 90 days, it might be important to limit the time during which the supply is drawn from the lake. For this purpose it would be necessary to employ gates (which would probably be the most expensive part of the work) along the line of the present summit level.

Two other locations for the connection between the lake and the river remain to be considered, one uniting the Great Calumet with the Kankakee, the other connecting the upper part of the Des Plaines with the lake. Whether either of these lines is suitable for an independent feeder or a navigable channel, can only be determined by special surveys.

The practical conclusion from the foregoing statement is, that a method of improvement by feeding from Lake Michigan as a reservoir is feasible between La Salle and Grafton, but above that point it will be necessary to employ locks and dams, and small sections of canal at Lockport, Joliet, and Marseilles rapids. The cost of such an improvement is indeterminate from the information at our command. It may be objected to by the theoretical deductions, that the quantity of water supposed to be supplied at the summit is the same as that determined by gauging the river at Hennepin, 110 miles lower down the river, and that the loss between those points may seriously affect the conclusions. This objection loses much of its importance when compared with the following facts:

The larger part of the river above La Salle flows over a rocky bed, and has but a small number of lagoons or sloughs along its borders to draw off water from the main body; that the lagoons once filled, the only additional quantity required would be for the purpose of supplying the losses from evaporation and infiltration, and that these losses might be met by increasing the period during which water is supplied to the river, rather than by increasing the actual discharge. The last statement is further strengthened by the fact that the low-water period, when a supply is required in the main river, seldom exceeds sixty or at most ninety days. By anticipating this period by several days the desired result might be attained.

* $V = 96 \ (rs) \ \frac{1}{2}.$

Although the union of the lakes with the Mississippi river is the great object sought, and the accomplishment of an almost uninterrupted navigation for this purpose is a desideratum, it must be remembered that the foregoing remarks are not conclusive in themselves, but rather indicate the importance of a thorough examination.

IV. LOCKS AND DAMS.

All methods of improvement applicable to rivers are feasible in the Illinois. But the characteristics of this stream are favorable to that system of improvement known as slack-water navigation, by-locks and dams. The fall per mile is so small that the construction of six dams is sufficient to overcome it, and to give a length of "pool" exceeding that of any known improvement of the same character. The dams may be so placed that no valuable land will be inundated. The deterioration of the river will be less than it is now in its present unimproved condition; the back flow of the dams will arrest the sediment brought down by affluents before it can reach the main body of the stream.

Medical writers attribute malarial fevers to the exhalation from decayed vegetable matter upon the surface of swamps and low grounds. The water of the pools covering the swamps and the low lands, exposed during the low-water period, with a broad sheet of pure water, will diminish this cause of disease.

Land owners entertain the opinion that valuable land will be injured by this method of improvement.

Inspection of the accompanying profile will remove apprehensions, so far as it relates to the ordinary navigable condition of the river. A little consideration will show that no damage can be effected by these structures at high water. During freshets, cultivated fields in the river bottoms are now submerged to a depth of from ten to fifteen feet. The increased velocity over the "combs" of the dams, compensating for a reduction in the inclination of the surface of the river, cannot seriously affect the discharge of the stream. But no injury can be done by the increase of the depth of water upon land already inundated. The dams may prolong the subsidence for ten hours, scarcely ever to the extent of twenty-four hours. The only serious cause of damage which can result from these structures must occur in the ordinary navigable condition of the river. This damage has been avoided by the selection of the sites of the proposed dams, and by dividing the entire fall into six "pools." The tendency of this method of improvement to increase the injury done at high water is more imaginary than real.

At Treetop bar, one and eight-tenths of a mile below La Salle, at low water, (giving twenty inches on the bar,) the discharge is about 633 cubic feet per second. The number of cubic feet of water required to pass a boat through a lock of the proposed dimensions is 196,785. The supply of water will, therefore, be sufficient to pass one boat every five minutes. But in case of extraordinary drought the lake summit of the Illinois and Michigan canal can be made to supply, at Lockport, any quantity of water that may be desired, the natural supply being double that required for ordinary purposes of navigation. The excess provided by artificial sources may be utilized for milling purposes.

Dimensions.—The Illinois and Michigan canal is 36 feet wide at bottom, 60 feet wide at top-water line, and has six feet depth of water; the locks are 110 feet long by 18 feet wide.

It is proposed to enlarge the canal so as to make an improvement of uniform dimensions between Lake Michigan and the Mississippi river.

In determining the dimensions to be given to the proposed improvement, the necessities of war and the more important wants of commerce should be taken into consideration. Any plan which would restrict the navigation to the low-water condition of the Mississippi river would fail to meet the wants of the grain-producing States. Economical transfer of freight can only be made by not breaking bulk ; the navigation should, therefore, be adapted to the largest class of river steamers.

Captain Ericsson has given the opinion that a "turreted monitor, bearing a 450-pound gun, can be built to draw not more than six and a half feet of water." A depth of seven and a half to eight feet of water, affording seven feet navigation, answering alike the wants of commerce, the necessities of war, and completing the connection between the lakes and the rivers of the west, would establish a harmonious commercial union with the best navigable condition of the Mississippi, the Missouri, the Ohio, and all their tributaries.

A plan of a lock to pass the largest class of river steamboats, or Ericsson's monitor, is herewith submitted. The length between the gates is 350 feet ; the width of the chamber is 75 feet. To reduce the cost the side walls are carried as high as the high-water mark from the head of the lock, to include the upper gates ; the remaining portion of the lock walls being raised eight feet above the comb of the dam. Whenever the water reaches this height locks will be unnecessary. It is proposed to construct the gates of boiler iron, and to move them in the simplest manner. The locks in every case resting on alluvial soil, the foundation must necessarily be expensive. It is proposed to rest the whole structure upon a massive bed of concrete, which will bind the walls together and settle uniformly.

Crib-dams, with stone filling and log foundation, such as have been adopted by experienced builders for rivers with a sandy bottom, have been estimated from the accompanying section.

Minute examination to determine definitely the best positions for locks and dams could not be made in a preliminary survey, but the sites selected have been carefully considered with reference to security of foundation, protection of the locks from ice, convenience of ingress and egress, and to give a minimum amount of dredging in the "pool" above. It is believed that the final determination will not differ materially from the positions indicated upon the profile.

The dams are named after the localities, and the locks have been numbered from the mouth of the river upwards.

Estimate of the cost of six dams and six locks between La Salle and the mouth of the river to give seven feet navigation, the lock being of sufficient dimensions to pass the largest class of river steamboats, viz., 350 feet between the gates, and 75 feet in width.

LOCK NUMBER ONE AND DAM AT SIX-MILE ISLAND.

10,385 cubic yards masonry, at $12 per yard................	$124,620 00
Slope wall, breast wall, and sill floor......................	5,826 00
11,891 cubic yards concrete foundation, at $6 per yard.......	71,346 00
Excavation of lock pit....................................	9,778 00
Coffer-dam, &c	27,380 00
Lock gates.......	30,000 00
1,440 lineal feet crib-dam and stone filling, complete..........	216,000 00
Dikes across sloughs.......	6,199 00
Cost of lock and dam...........................	491,149 00

LOCK NUMBER TWO AND DAM AT COLUMBIANA.

The locks not being built to be used at high water, and having the same soil for foundation, small variation in cost can occur from a difference of lift or from the variable substratum upon which they will rest ; this cost is assumed as constant.

Cost of lock No. 2..	$268,950	00
Abutments and slope walls...............................	4,796	00
1,240 feet of dam, (no dikes required)...................	186,000	00
Cost of lock and dam.............................	459,746	00

LOCK NUMBER THREE AND THE NAPLES DAM.

Cost of lock..	$268,950	00
880 lineal feet of dam....................................	132,000	00
Abutments and slope walls...............................	4,796	00
Cost of lock and dam.............................	405,746	00

LOCK NUMBER FOUR AND DAM AT FREDERICK.

Cost of lock...............................	$268,950	00
980 lineal feet of dam...................................	147,000	00
Abutments and slope walls...............................	4,796	00
Cost of lock and dam.............................	430,746	00

LOCK NUMBER FIVE AND DAM AT SPRING LAKE.

Cost of lock..	$268,950	00
800 lineal feet of dam....................................	120,000	00
Abutments and slope walls...............................	4,796	00
Dikes across slough......................................	876	00
Cost of lock and dam.............................	394,622	00

LOCK NUMBER SIX AND DAM AT CHILLICOTHE.

Cost of lock..	$268,950	00
930 lineal feet of dam....................................	139,500	00
Abutments and slope walls...............................	4,796	00
Dikes across sloughs....................................	2,442	00
Cost of lock and dam.............................	415,688	00

Recapitulation of the cost of six dams and six locks for the Illinois river, between La Salle and its mouth, designed to give seven feet navigation; the locks to be 350 feet between mitre-sills, and 75 feet wide in the chamber.

Names of locks and dams.	Lift.	Height of dam.	Length of dam.	Length of pools.	Cost of construction.
	Feet.	Feet.	Feet.	Miles.	
Six-mile island dam and lock No. 1	4.0	11.0	1,440	25½	$491,149 00
Columbiana dam and lock No. 2.	4.0	8.0	1,240	28	459,746 00
Naples dam and lock No. 3	5.0	9.5	880	25¼	405,746 00
Frederick dam and lock No. 4..	5.8	10.3	950	43½	420,746 00
Spring Lake dam and lock No. 5.	5.7	10.8	800	49¼	394,622 00
Chillicothe dam and lock No. 6.	7.5	14.0	930	42 44/100	415,688 00
Total					2,587,697 00

Total cost for construction	$2,587,697 00
Add for dredging 200,000 cubic yards, transporting material, &c.	250,000 00
Add for drainage to land and contingencies	286,099 00
Cost of lock and dam improvement	3,123,796 00

V. ESTIMATE FOR ENLARGING THE ILLINOIS AND MICHIGAN CANAL.

In further compliance with your instructions, I herewith submit an approximate estimate of the cost of enlarging the Illinois and Michigan canal, to constitute, with the improvement of the river below La Salle, a water communication of uniform depth between Lake Michigan and the Mississippi river. In making this estimate I am obliged to depend exclusively upon information furnished by the courtesy of Mr. Gooding, secretary of the Illinois and Michigan Canal Company.

Material drawn from the carefully constructed map and profile sent to you by this gentleman, together with information found in such reports and letters as were available, afford the bases for the statements accompanying this estimate. The distance from La Salle to Chicago is ninety-seven miles. It is proposed to cut down the present summit to the low-water level of the lake, and to give a depth of seven feet to the new channel.

With the exception of short canals between Lockport and Joliet, and at the Marseilles rapids, it is deemed advisable to abandon the old location, and to improve the natural channel of the river by locks and dams. This plan will be less expensive than the enlargement of the original canal. Between Lockport and La Salle, the average fall per mile is 1.4 foot. The actual fall at the following named places is much greater:

At Lockport, there is a lockage of fifty feet in 6.7 miles; at Joliet, there is a lockage of thirty-two and a half feet in a distance of nine and a half miles; and at the Marseilles rapids the lockage is thirty-six feet in ten miles; the entire lockage to reach the mouth of the river would be 170 feet in 321 miles.

For a canal from Bridgeport (four and a half miles from Chicago) to Lockport, twenty-nine miles long, and 160 feet wide, having a depth of seven feet, constituting the proposed lake summit level, the following quantities and prices have been politely furnished by Mr. Gooding:

10,500,000 cubic yards of earth excavation, at 50 cents	$5,250,000
500,000 cubic yards of rock excavation, at $2	1,000,000
1,000,000 cubic yards of bank excavation, at 25 cents	250,000
2,000,000 cubic yards of rock excavation, at $1 25	2,500,000
316,000 cubic yards of walling, at $3	948,000
Banks, gates, waste-weirs, &c	150,000
Total	10,098,000

Without giving, says Mr. Gooding, a detailed estimate of the cost of the improvement from Lockport to La Salle, I think, after looking over the items which went to make up the former estimate, it is safe to say the cost would not now exceed $6,000,000.

The cost of making a water communication between Lake Michigan and the proposed improvement of the Illinois river below La Salle will be, according to Mr. Gooding, $16,098,000.

The same quantities, however, have been estimated at prices furnished by experienced contractors. In one case, the total cost would be $18,216,810; another set of prices gives the sum of $23,575,000. To either of these estimates, $3,123,796 should be added in order to obtain the cost of a continuous improvement to the mouth of the river.

Assuming the second estimate as the one nearest the true cost, the sum is much less than could be expected.

The Oswego branch of the Erie canal, adapted for ordinary canal-boats, cost rather more than $80,000 per mile; the Erie canal, built for the same class of boats, cost $91,000 per mile—its total cost exceeding $30,000,000.

The Illinois river improvement, including the enlargement of the Illinois and Michigan canal, admitting the passage of the largest class of river steamers, would cost, according to the foregoing estimate, about $68,000 per mile; and the entire cost would be $21,339,996.

VI.—*The following table furnishes data for making a comparison between the cost and dimensions of some of the more important canals in the United States and Canada:*

Names of canals.	Size of locks.	Am't of lockage.	Length in miles.	Cost per mile.	Total cost.
Erie canal	110×18	654.8	363	....	$33,033,000 00
Oswego branch	110×18	155	38	$80,984 00	3,077,392 00
St. Lawrence canals, having three classes of locks	200×45 142×40 180×26½	205½	43¾	104,100 00	4,515,337 50
Welland canal	200×45	33	28	232,142 00	6,499,976 00
Chesapeake and Ohio canal	100×18	610	165	59,618 00	11,071,176 00
Illinois and Michigan canal	110×18	138	96		
Proposed Illinois river improvement	350×75	32	224	13,945 51	3,123,796 00

STATISTICAL.

It may not be out of place before closing this report to bring together a few facts which establish the superiority of the Illinois river as the route for a navigable connection between the lakes and the Mississippi river. Some of the arguments drawn from these facts, applying with almost equal force to all the routes proposed for affecting this object, demonstrate the importance of opening every practicable communication between the east and the west. The line of the Illinois possesses the following advantages:

The sources of the river being in a lower latitude than any of its rivals, this advantage increases as the river advances in its course, and, as a consequence, less obstruction to navigation, and less damage to works of improvement may be anticipated from the length of the winter and the breaking up of ice in the spring. Being by nature more favorable to improvement, navigation can be established upon it and maintained at less cost. It alone, of all the proposed routes, passes along extensive coal beds, affording convenient fuel for steamers.*

The same coal measures supply Chicago and the thriving cities upon the river, and are destined to play a more important part in the development of the north-west. Wool from Wisconsin and Iowa, and cotton from Memphis and New Orleans, may be brought to the doors of factories on the banks of the Illinois river. Possessing the rare advantage of producing in abundance both food and fuel, here must spring up a manufacturing population, which, in progress of time, will furnish the domestic fabrics and clothing for the inhabitants of the valley of the Mississippi.

---

* Coal is found on the lower Rock river.

The upper Mississippi and Missouri, draining an area of 687,000 square miles, unite near the southern terminus of the proposed improvement.

A more important advantage belongs to the valley of the Illinois ; upon it alone is a navigation practicable for the largest steamers, by the completion of which a union will be effected with the best navigable condition of the western rivers, possessing an aggregate length in their main channels of 12,000 miles, exceeding in their collateral channels and tributaries 39,000 miles, and draining an area of 911,000 square miles, with 90,300 square miles of lake surface, bearing a commerce of 413,000 tons burden.

It possesses another advantage, almost exclusively its own. The two most opulent cities of the west are found at its termini. The revenue collected at the port of St. Louis in 1866 amounted to $835,012. The revenue collected at Chicago, though much larger, is not known. The amount collected for the tonnage, admeasurement, and enrolling of boats plying on the Illinois and Michigan canal was $9,000.

Notwithstanding the suspension of navigation by low water for two months, 477 steamers arrived at St. Louis during the past year, and the tolls on the Illinois and Michigan canal, accruing from the same source during the same period, amounted to $302,000.

Although the coal trade has just begun, 21,000 tons were sent to Chicago alone in 1866. How much was sent elsewhere I have no means of determining.

A list is appended showing the articles and quantities arriving at St. Louis and Chicago by this route. The important way trade has not been ascertained, but that this must be considerable is evident from the existence of the flourishing cities of Lacon, Henry, Chillicothe, Peoria, Pekin, Beardstown, and Naples.

The real importance of this improvement can only be estimated by regarding it as completing a system of water communication between the east and the west, of which the Oswego and Erie canals constitute essential parts. Statistical reports of boards of trade, and the report of the Chicago convention, contain some interesting facts illustrating this view of the subject. They show that by cheapening transportation the improvement will make an immense extent of country accessible to New York and Chicago. The saving in the cost of transportation to be effected by the enlargement of the Illinois and Michigan canal, and the improvement of the Illinois river, is shown to be one-half as compared with summer rates, and two-thirds of winter rates. These rates amount to a prohibition on corn grown 100 miles west of Chicago. It appears from the same statement that the gross amount of 550,000,000 bushels of cereals was produced by the eight food-producing States of the northwest.

The mining population of Lake Superior consumes 150,000 bushels of cereals annually. The shipment of copper from that quarter in 1862 amounted to 10,000 tons, valued at $4,000,000. The iron from the same region amounted to 414,000 tons. The resources of the vast region tributary to this system of improvement would require a volume to illustrate its extent.

The Mississippi has ceased to be the great outlet for the trade of this region ; the heat of tropical seas, an unhealthy climate, and a détour of 3,000 miles from a direct line to the markets of the world, have diverted the flow of animal and vegetable food. The exports from New Orleans before the war, in the article of wheat, did not exceed the annual receipts of Milwaukee and Toledo.

As a part of the communication between the Atlantic and Pacific, this route derives additional importance. The completion of 220 miles of improvement will afford steam navigation during six or seven months of the year, from the Atlantic ocean to Omaha, on the Missouri, nearly one-half the distance between the two oceans. California, with an annual gold product valued at $100,000,000, will pay the largest tribute to the route affording the greatest facilities.

The present course of trade leaves little doubt what that route would be.

The recent establishment of a line of steamers between China, Japan, and San Francisco will lead to a diversion of a great part of that valuable trade to our Pacific coast. The Pacific railroad will then bring Chicago and the northwestern lakes into commercial union with the East Indies, and that trade, which has hitherto conferred commercial supremacy, will transfer a portion of its benefits upon the valley of the Mississippi.

Very respectfully, your obedient servant,

S. T. ABERT.

Brevet Maj. Gen. J. H. WILSON, U. S. A.,
　　Lieut. Colonel 35th U. S. Infantry.

Table of the principal articles exported and imported on the Illinois and Michigan canal, and entered at the Chicago collector's office, for the years 1865 and 1866.

Articles.	Cleared.		Arrived.	
	1865.	1866.	1865.	1866.
Flour ....barrels..	700	1,651	55,216	45,317
Fish ....do....	105	218	7	5
Lime, common ....do....	1,718	2,243	311	192
Lime, hydraulic ....do....	334	349	632	1,066
Oil ....do....	429	154	53	15
Pork ....do....	1,167	82	6,143	3,340
Salt ....do....	76,809	30,697	458	2
Whiskey...................do....	558	72	2,028	583
Barley ....bushels..	275,546	4,491	13,850	24,961
Beans ....do....	20	60	1,096	306
Buckwheat..................do....	....	20	....	26
Corn ....do....	....	125,555	8,639,109	9,575,569
Oats ....do....	296,627	99,132	1,145,363	1,417,436
Peas ....do....	164	13	....	....
Potatoes ....do....	1,009	1,233	1,800	2,576
Rye ....do....	8,683	3,586	102,594	67,423
Wheat......................do....	246,284	235,758	260,058	83,834
Onions ....do....	....	261	....	....
Agricultural implements...pounds..	163,246	78,362	58,919	22,780
Butter ....do....	....	....	142,404	18,610
Brooms ....do....	....	6,000	....	8,189
Bacon ....do....	....	....	105,760	36,868
Broom-corn ....do....	....	....	91,260	9,130
Bran and shorts............do....	42,255	30,072	725,806	1,560,596
Bacon, farmers'............do....	1,929,037	2,439,108	....	....
Joiners' work..............do....	93,291	90,508	16,876	7,800
Stone coal.................do....	5,869,407	8,687,596	30,119,220	47,222,050
Drainage pipe ....do....	....	....	1,064,748	1,574,969
Eggs ....do....	....	....	25,296	12,800
Empty barrels ....do....	121,270	14,121	2,772,862	2,317,831
Glass ....do....	....	20,000	....	22,426
Hides ....do....	....	....	306,531	36,966
Hams ....do....	....	....	55,456	109,145
Iron ....do....	3,105,318	912,425	215,795	98,518
Ice ....do....	160,000	....	....	....
Leather ....do....	12,327	4,899	5,294	....
Lard ....do....	....	....	189,702	298,490
Merchandise................do....	1,158,414	808,098	37,294	19,268
Molasses ....do....	4,900	7,835	18,530	13,160
Machinery ....do....	213,429	170,386	....	89,380
Nails and spikes ....do....	274,634	102,760	....	6,140
Powder ....do....	38,484	8,705	....	1,100

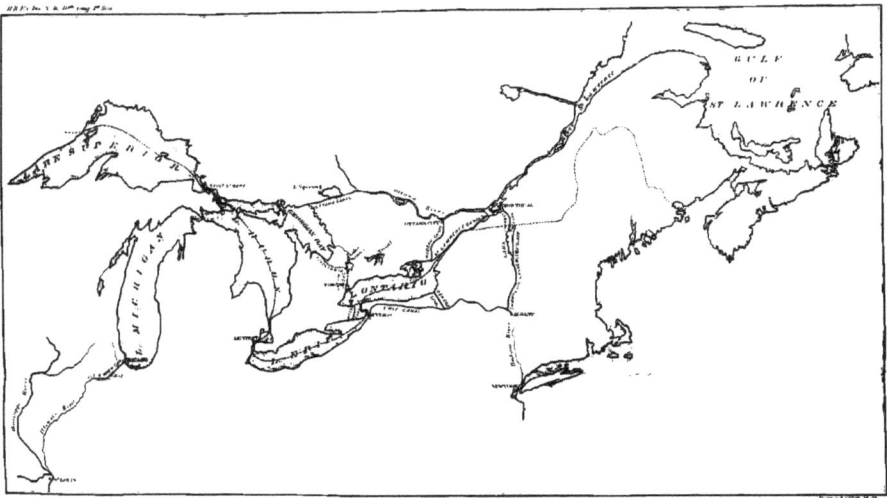

Principal articles exported and imported, &c.—Continued.

Articles.	Cleared.		Arrived.	
	1865.	1866.	1865.	1866.
ovisions .... pounds..	....	....	245,065	5,120
,tters' ware ....do	72,099	134,445	....	....
igar ....do	210,974	96,568	....	....
.taves ....do	1,953,204	6,394,636	....	609,140
.tarch ....do	1,296	....	749,702	1,122,776
.eeds ....do	....	23,955	775,157	1,246,209
Tallow ....do	....	....	62,702	33,067
Wool ....do	....	3,343	87,566	82,924
Brick...................number..	29,130	841,575	....	844,400
.ath ....do	7,855,415	8,359,955	....	59,100
.hingles ....do....	29,289,600	19,392,500	....	119,250
.ence posts...... ,.........do	96,755	70,866	....	350
.umber.............feet, b. m..	77,794,095	67,951,954	....	465,315
.ling ....do....	1,261,151	730,948	....	42,114
,oring, dressed ....do....	....	739,122	....	8,854
.nber................cubic feet..	8,373	22,542	....	1,400
.one............cubic yards..	....	71,877	58,486	82,334
Wood ....cords....	758	710	924	1,171
Canal-boats......number of miles..	186,750	209,855	188,400	225,910

Receipts from the Illinois river at St. Louis, for the years 1865 *and* 1866.

Articles.	1865.	1866.
Apples .... barrels..	16,660	21,773
Bacon..................................casks and tierces..	826	1,629
Bacon ....packages..	583	233
'acon ....pieces..	2,899	19,770
rley ....sacks..	12,010	....
rley....................................bushels..	297,645	55,921
aus ....sacks..	341	668
aus ....barrels..	205	225
:f ....barrels..	338	....
.n ....sacks..	22,492	31,994
.oms...................................dozen..	9,823	5,484
.om-corn ....bales..	44	605
.ter....................................packages..	572	1,454
C.tle ....head..	2,552	2,623
Ce.ent ....barrels..	1,478	3,443
Coperage ....flour barrels..	2,818	1,676
Operage ....pork and lard barrels..	3,962	13,686
f.n ....sacks..	536,739	....
C.n ....bushels..	205,854	2,607,235
.rn meal ....sacks..	1,415	184
Corn meal ....barrels..	3,905	3,181
Eggs ....boxes..	455	894
.lax-seed ....sacks..	1,026	3,858
Fish ....barrels..	1,088	93
Flour ....sacks..	52,243	16,993
Flour ....barrels..	146,769	135,353
Hay ....bales..	48,875	3,977
Hardware ....packages..	....	2,722
Stoves ....pieces..	....	367
Ship stuff..............................sacks..	804	578
Starch ....boxes..	1,205	3,140
Shingles ....M..	....	2,210

Receipts from the Illinois river at St. Louis—Continued.

Articles.	1865.	1866.
Tallow ....tierces...	150	109
Tallow ....barrels...	1,033	712
Tobacco...hogsheads...	32	79
Tobacco...boxes...	110	289
Tobacco...packages...	357	263
Hemp ....bales...	61	285
Hides...pieces...	5,280	2,978
Hides...bales...	402	345
Hogs ....head...	4,402	7,548
Iron..tons...	....	101
Lard ....tierces...	3,219	1,403
Lard ....barrels...	869	341
Lard ....packages...	740	1,570
Lead ....pigs...	....	274
Lime..barrels...	200	1,826
Leather...rolls...	72	265
Lumber ....feet, b. m...	51,862,730	45,301,300
Merchandise......................................packages...	....	72,188
Oats..bushels...	1,735,575	985,230
Onions ....sacks...	6,756	2,092
Onions ....barrels...	787	1,083
Pork ....do...	23,289	14,442
Pork ....packages...	2,925	538
Pork ....pieces...	56,388	47,989
Potatoes ....sacks...	64,760	78,629
Potatoes ....barrels...	8,158	11,976
Rope ....coils...	973	74
Rags..packages...	1,866	809
Rye ....bushels...	63,004	168,678
Salt ....sacks...	28,969	4,418
Salt ....barrels...	107,567	61,731
Seed ....sacks...	481	1,902
Sheep ....head...	2,314	4,332
Tar and pitch ....barrels...	....	693
Wheat ....sacks...	352,724	....
Wheat ....barrels...	9,698	....
Wheat ....bushels...	128,873	608,092
Whiskey ....barrels...	13,647	16,866
Wines ....do...	....	605
Wines ....cases...	....	358
Wool ....packages...	87	63
White lead ....kegs...	....	706

Arrivals of steamboats from Illinois river in 1865... 57
Departures of steamboats from Illinois river in 1865.. 77
Arrivals of steamboats from Illinois river in 1866.. 54

Extracts from "The Canadian Canals, &c.," by Mr. W. Kingsford, C. E.

The produce of the west, limited only by the means of transportation to its natural market, the Atlantic borders, has but two avenues to its destination, the Hudson and the St. Lawrence rivers, both of which can only be reached by artificial water communication. The relative merits of these can be understood only by a detailed description of each, which is furnished by Mr. W. Kingsford, in his "Canadian Canals," from which the following data are extracted:

I. THE CANADIAN CANALS.

The canal system of Canada may be described under four heads:

1. The Chambly canal, connecting the waters of the Saint Lawrence with

the Hudson river, at Waterford, through the Richelieu, Lake Champlain, and the Whitehall canal.

2. The Rideau canal, connecting Lake Ontario, at Kingston, with the Ottawa river, at Bytown, now called Ottawa, and so by the Grenville and Carillon canals with the Saint Lawrence, at the island of Montreal, by the well-known Saint Anne's lock.

3. The Saint Lawrence canals, by which the Saint Lawrence is itself made navigable.

4. The Welland canal, making a connection between Lakes Ontario and Erie.

Leaving out of consideration the Chambly canal, as entirely out of the way of western trade, and the Rideau canal, constructed in the primary view of the defence of the province, and made commercially unimportant by the completion of the Saint Lawrence route, we turn at once to the Saint Lawrence canals.

These very important works, the locks which connect the western lakes through the Saint Lawrence with the seaboard at Montreal, are as follows :

1. The Lachine canal, 5 locks, mean rise........ 44¾ feet; length 8½ miles.
2. The Beauharnois canal, 9 locks, mean rise..... 82½   11¼
3. The Cornwall canal, 6 locks, mean rise........ 48   11½
4. Williamsburg—
    Farren's Point, 1 lock, mean rise........... 4   ¾
    Rapide Plat, 2 locks, mean rise........... 11½   3¾
    Iroquois, ⎫
    Junction, ⎬ 3 locks, mean rise............ 15¾   7⅝
    Gallops, ⎭

                                                             43¾

Including, for comparison—
The Welland canal, 27 locks, mean rise......... 330 feet; length 28 miles.
Fall on portions of the Saint Lawrence not requir-
    ing locks 15¾
Height of Lake Erie above Montreal harbor...... 551¾
Add for difference of level between Montreal and
    tide-water—Three Rivers.................. 12¾
Difference of level between tide-water and Lake
    Erie 564½

The size of the locks of all the canals between Montreal and Lake Ontario is 200 feet by 45 feet, with 9 feet of water on the sills. Cornwall canal is the exception, being 54 feet wide at the surface; but in the lower level the dimensions are contracted to a width of 42 feet.

The Welland canal, from Port Dalhousie to St. Catherines, has three locks, 200 feet by 45 feet, with 10 feet water on the sills, and the entrance locks of the main canal at Port Colborn, and the feeder at Port Maitland, have each a length of 200 feet, with a width of 45 feet. The remainder are 150 feet by 26 feet 6 inches in width, with 10 feet water on sills.

Thus it is evident, while the Saint Lawrence canals proper can pass vessels of greater tonnage capacity than those which can navigate the Welland, that the latter, having one foot more draught, must be lightened to that extent before they can pass through the Saint Lawrence canals.

Lachine canal.—The Lachine canal was, perhaps, the earliest great work proposed after the conquest, and its necessity was advocated before the passage of the constitutional act in 1791.

In 1815 the exigencies of the war in the transport of munitions led the governor general, Sir George Provost, to recommend its execution, but peace came and no further effort was made. The present width of the canal is 80 feet at bottom and 120 feet at top

It is officially asserted that the expenditure for repairs and maintenance is much larger on this than the other canals. The mill-sites sold by the government, and which are now worked, take so great a supply of water that a strong current runs throughout its length.

The same results consequently occur as arise in natural rivers. The banks are washed in spite of their protection walls, and bars are formed in the channels and basins. The dredging machine is accordingly in constant requisition.

Beauharnois canal.—The Beauharnois canal succeeded, as a consequence, in the improvement of the navigation. Its length is $11\frac{1}{2}$ miles, with 9 locks to overcome $82\frac{1}{2}$ feet of level. Its outlet, at Beauharnois, in Lake Saint Louis, is distant about 19 miles of navigable water from the entrance of the Lachine canal, and accordingly it connects the above lake with Lake St. Francis. The impediments overcome are the well-known Cascades, Cedars, and Coteau rapids. Between these several interruptions to the navigation, there are reaches of still water, and it would not have been impossible to have constructed three separate small canals, and to have passed to the quiet water and abandoned the river where it ceased. But such plans for an incomplete result really save little money, and give imperfect satisfaction, from the impediments and delays in navigation which they fail to remove. This canal, thrown at once across the land, and in one work overcoming all the obstacles to be dealt with, may be adduced as an example of successful engineering of the more enlarged school.

Cornwall canal.—The distance between the entrance of the Beauharnois and the discharge of the Cornwall canal is 40 miles of a good and well marked out channel. The Cornwall canal was constructed to avoid the Longue Sault rapids. It is $11\frac{1}{2}$ miles long, with a rise of 48 feet. It has 6 lift locks, and a guard lock. The locks are 54 feet wide between the quoins, but the decreasing capacity in the lower chamber really limits them to paddle-wheel steamers of 49 feet width, and this is 5 feet in excess of the other canals.

Williamsburg canals.—These canals were originally four in number, and although contemplated at the time of the commencement of the Cornwall canal, they were not begun until 1843.

The first in the series is the Farren's Point lock, 4.9 miles distant from the Cornwall canal. It is three-quarters of a mile long, with a lift of 4 feet. Ten miles higher occurs the Rapide Flat canal, 3.9 miles long, with 11.6 feet lift, on which is a guard and a lift lock.

Four and a half miles higher are the two upper canals, united by the junction, and forming one canal. It escapes the Gallops and Iroquois rapids. There are two lift locks and a guard lock. The rise is 15.9 feet, the length $7\frac{3}{5}$ miles. The distance from the latter to Prescott is $6\frac{5}{9}$ miles. These canals have only 50 feet at bottom. The rapids which they overcome are comparatively slight, and are navigated both ways by passenger steamers. Accordingly these canals are principally used by upward bound freight craft.

The Welland canal.—The Welland canal connects Lake Ontario and Erie, carrying the navigation around the rapids and the renowned Falls of Niagara. It is 28 miles in length, with 27 locks, rising to an upper level of 330 feet. The three locks, from the outlet at Port Dalhousie, on Lake Ontario, to Saint Catherines, a distance of 4 miles, are 200 feet by 45 feet, by which means Saint Catherines has been made the head of the Saint Lawrence navigation, and would accordingly claim to be considered in any project of improvement of the Saint Lawrence canals. The remaining 24 locks are 180 feet by 26.6 feet, except the guard lock at Port Colborn, Lake Erie, which is 240 feet by 45 feet. The guard lock to the feeder at Port Maitland is of similar dimensions. The original depth on the sills of the enlarged canal was 9 feet, but as great difficulty was experienced during some years in passing the largest class of deeply laden vessels, it was decided, in 1853, to increase the draught of water to 10 feet. This was effected in that year by raising and strengthening the banks.

The present position of this canal is, that it is utterly insufficient for the trade which passes through it. That it must be widened and deepened, and that the locks must be enlarged, is admitted, if it is to become equal to the requirements upon it. Even should the policy of deepening the whole series of canals be rejected, the Welland must be improved. The question is, to what extent should the enlargement be made? It is urged that much of the craft of Lake Erie cannot now pass the canal to Lake Ontario; but the argument in this form has no great force. There is a navigation peculiar to Lake Erie, which is not met with on Lake Ontario, and the limit to be applied to the western canal must be sought in the Saint Lawrence, and not in the upper lakes, and here we have no identity of view.

Be the dimensions what they may, the necessity must be recognized, that two vessels navigating the canal may pass at any part of it; hence the width at the bottom must be at least 100 feet.

PROJECTED WORKS.

From the constructed canals we turn to those projects which are advocated as essential improvements, and which have been brought pointedly before the public:

Ottaway and French river navigation.

The first in magnitude is the Ottawa canal, which was made known in 1858, by the full and carefully written report of Mr. Walter Shanly. It is proposed to pass from Lake Huron up the French river to Lake Nippissinque, to construct a canal across the water-shed of the Saint Lawrence and Ottawa into Trout lake, at the head of the Matawan, (a tributary of the Ottawa,) and to follow that stream to the junction of the two rivers; then to turn into the Ottawa and to follow its course to the island of Montreal. The supply was proposed to be taken from Lake Nippissinque, raised by dams to the height of Trout lake, twenty-three feet higher than its natural level—" at once increasing the storage capacity of the summit from twelve to upwards of three hundred square miles." The rapids on the route Mr. Shanly proposed to throw back by dams, introducing locks where necessary to overcome the difference of level of these artificial reaches. The French river, like the tributaries of the Ottawa, and that river itself, is not navigable, owing to the various rapids which intervene. These various impediments would be removed by eight dams and one mile of canal navigation. The number of locks would be eight, overcoming sixty-seven feet. Lake Nippissinque, it is estimated, would need three dams. To pass the summit would require a canal of five miles, with a maximum cut of thirty feet through granite rock, overcoming sixteen feet of a lift by two locks, the summit level being eighty-three feet above Lake Huron, in a distance of eighty-five miles.

Descending the Matawan, the distance, 40.42 miles in length, would consist of 30.66 miles by river, and 9.76 miles by canal; 170 feet of descent would be overcome by eighteen locks, and thirteen dams would be necessary to control and assure the navigation.

Descending the Ottawa to the city of Ottawa, we have a distance of 195 miles, of which only twenty-two miles are canal navigation. The descent is 376 feet to the basin, from whence ascend the tier of locks to the Rideau canal. Mr. Shanly's estimate of the work is $24,000,000.

He does not " venture to calculate on more than 180 days' navigation," considering Sunday *dies non.* Adding one-sixth to his figures will give 210 days which may be considered as from fifteen to twenty days less than the navigation on the Saint Lawrence route.

From Ottawa to the Lachine canal, a long series of works and improvements will be required. The present Greenville and Carillon canals being quite valueless for the upper limit of navigation, improvements will be necessary in both the Ottawa and Saint Lawrence.

The geographical situation of this navigation can only have in view the trade of Lake Michigan, for from the lakes east of these waters the nearest route is by the Saint Lawrence, hence the comparison is narrower to the distance between Chicago and Montreal.

It is as follows :

By the Welland and Saint Lawrence canals, the distance is..... 1,348 miles.
By the Ottawa route. .... ' 980

Therefore, by the Saint Lawrence there is an excess of......... 368

And upon this it is estimated that the time taken on the former route would be 196 hours ; on the latter, 152 hours. Mr. Shanly estimates the reduction of the cost of transportation per ton at thirty-seven cents. He avoids all the Saint Lawrence canals except the Lachine. It is somewhat hard to see how the cost of transport by the Ottawa will be less than by the existing route. If tolls be affected at all by outlay (as a rule they are a matter of expediency) the tolls of the Ottawa route would be fully as high as those of the Saint Lawrence canals, even when improved, for it is considered that twelve millions would effect all the changes which the most unflinching advocate of the advantages of the lakes and river would exact. This sum, added to the thirteen millions, the cost of the Welland and Saint Lawrence canals, would be the outlay for the Ottawa route, and accordingly it should exact about the same tolls. The Ottawa canal offers no one ground to hope for an increase of traffic from fresh channels of trade, because it does not contemplate more than the delivery of freights at Montreal. At this moment, the drawback in the Saint Lawrence route, which virtually destroys its importance, only appears at the foot of the canals. It is well known that while the present relations in trade prevail ocean freights from Montreal will continue high ; and this difficulty, without a radical alteration in the whole character of the western commerce, is insurmountable. The weak point in the Ottawa project is, that it neither considers the fact nor in any way creates the remedy. Were it carried out, if the theory of its excellence be correct, it would injuriously affect many interests of western Canada without one compensating benefit, or one single national advantage.

Toronto and Georgian Bay canal.

Of late years a connection by canal between Georgian bay (an inlet of Lake Huron) and Toronto has been frequently advocated. At this moment it is prominently before the public, and the propriety of its construction is forcibly urged, with something of an organization. The estimated length is 100 miles. The course would run from the mouth of the river Humber, about five miles west of Toronto, and there ascend the river in a northerly direction to the level of Lake Simcoe, 470 feet above Lake Ontario, crossing by canal the dividing ridge which separates it from the Holland river, by which it would continue on the same level to the lake. An open navigation of twenty-three miles would cross Lake Simcoe to Kempenfeldt bay, near Barrie, whence a communication would extend to the Nottawasaga river, by which it would descend to Lake Huron, 130 feet below Lake Simcoe—the size of the locks to be 265 feet long, fifty-five feet in width, and twelve feet lift. This width would allow two schooners of 400 tons each to pass through at the same time. It is now nearly twenty years since

Mr. Kivas Tully first made an exploration of the line of the proposed canal. On a second occasion, in 1851, he ran a line of levels to ascertain the elevation of the "ridges" which form the water-shed between Lakes Simcoe and Ontario. Mr. Tully at once saw the difficulties to be encountered and the immense probable cost, and the subject was allowed to drop. Lately it has been revived, and its promoters urge that the increase of the population of the western States, and the consequent advance in agricultural wealth and commercial enterprise, call for increased canal accommodation. That independently of the positive view of benefits obtained, the loss of life and property on the Saint Clair flats and Lake Erie is so great that a large expenditure would be warranted in order to insure the avoidance of such disasters. On the 14th of September, 1855, a convention of delegates from the cities of Chicago, Milwaukee, Oswego, and Toronto, and the towns of Barrie and Orillia, met at Toronto, when the following resolution was unanimously adopted :

"That the immense trade from the northwest demands the immediate construction of a canal between the upper lakes and Lake Ontario, of sufficient capacity to pass vessels of one thousand tons burden from Lake Huron to Lake Ontario, at Toronto, or its vicinity."

According to Mr. Tully's calculations, the Georgian Bay canal, if constructed, would effect a saving in distance between Chicago and Liverpool of 837 miles, as compared with the route by Buffalo and the Erie canal to New York, and 428 miles less than the route by the Welland canal to Quebec; the saving in time to New York being, by Oswego, fifty hours, as compared with the Buffalo route, and to Quebec thirty-six hours, as compared with the Welland route ; no notice being taken of the detention in passing the St. Clair flats, which may be estimated at three days each way. It is further urged, that the average annual losses to shipping in the St. Clair flats and Lake Erie may be taken at $1,000,000. The detention and loss in passing the St. Clair flats attracted so much attention, that a charter was obtained, in 1857, for the construction of a ship canal from the St. Clair river to Rondeau, an estimated distance of thirty-six miles, to save 131 miles of hazardous navigation.

Mr. Tully has in no way concealed the formidable character of the undertaking of crossing the ridge. The cutting extends for ten miles, averaging throughout ninety feet in depth. It gradually rises to a height of 200 feet on a base of this length, and the apex of the triangle in the section is towards Lake Simcoe. Between Lakes Simcoe and Huron, the work extends six and a half miles with a cutting of fifty feet. Lake Simcoe is 130 feet above Lake Huron, and 475 feet above Lake Ontario. It is a large body of water, with many tributaries, and the question has not been raised that it would be insufficient for the supply.

The various projects have been placed side by side, so that we can judge of their several characteristics. Dispassionate criticism cannot assign to any of them a place in a well considered provincial policy. There is not one which can command more than local support, for there is not one which, if consummated, will have any extended influence on the trade of the province, and, with one exception, they may be dismissed as having failed to impress public opinion.

That exception is the Ottawa route, supported by the wealth of Montreal, and from the influence and high character of its advocates, almost certain to obtain universal favor in eastern Canada. It must be opposed by western Canada without compromise, as secondary to the necessity of extending the navigation of the St. Lawrence. *Latterly, it has been advocated under what are termed its military aspects.* The arguments advanced to sustain this view are as fallacious as the complaint uttered at the Chicago convention, of the defenceless condition of the Lake Erie cities. Should war ever occur between England and the United States, and Canada be made the battle-ground, we may expect that on both sides the canals would soon be rendered useless. The incidental use of the military argument is to give importance to this route, the true value of which is commercial.

There is only one line of policy to be adopted with regard to the canals. Our course of action is suggested by the magnitude of the trade of the western States, which, if turned into its natural outlet, the St. Lawrence, would lead to the important results all yearn to effect. *We can gain this trade, if we improve the St. Lawrence and deepen the canals to fifteen feet, and construct a chain of locks 250 feet by 45 feet wide. Here is the true policy for us to pursue; if we fail to follow it, we neglect every advantage, geographical and commercial, which we possess.*

The Erie canal.

The importance of this work, the great part it has acted in the settlement of the lake States, and the position which it occupies in relation to the Canadian canals in the competition for the carrying trade of the northwest, suggests the inquiry, if it has reached its maximum development, and if the accommodation it extends can be increased. It is not to be expected that a diversion of the trade from the Hudson would be effected without a great effort on the part of New York to retain it, and such effort would take the form of increasing the Erie canal, if possible to do so. No expense would be spared to create a channel for commerce which should extend every requirement sought for, and which, by the advantages it possessed, would have the effect of preventing that commerce from seeking other favorable routes. The only course open to New York to draw within the State the trade of the west, and to enjoy the manifold benefits which are blended with it, is to create a route to the sea as a whole without a rival, and which it would be a matter of necessity, for it would be a matter of interest, to pursue.

There is no such thing as nationality in trade. Produce from the west will seek the east by the most profitable route, and there is no legislation which can interfere with the St. Lawrence, so long as it is free to the flags of all nations, and at the same time offers the greatest inducements for freight to follow it. The canal system of New York is wonderful in extent; a description of it is a history in itself. The relations of the west, however, are confined to the Erie canal and the Oswego branch, and it is on their efficiency as channels for produce that the cost of transport depends. *It is notorious that their present dimensions are unequal to the trade,* and propositions have been put forward to increase the size of the locks, in order to admit vessels of greater tonnage, and by these means reduce the cost of freight and lessen the period of navigation.

The Erie canal has its entrance at Buffalo, and passes along the Niagara river some twelve miles to the entrance to Tonawanda creek, which has a width of 200 feet, with a depth of 9 feet. It follows the creek, on the Lake Erie level, to Pendleton, where the canal proper commences; but no change is made in the level for a further distance of seven miles, to Lockport, where the first descent is made, 56 feet, by five combined locks. This reach is continued a distance of 31 miles, to Rochester, 93 miles from Buffalo, and 7 from Lake Ontario, above the height of which the canal here is 265 feet. Independent of the Lockport lockage, the upper waters of Tonawanda creek are forced into Oak Orchard creek, and by the latter passed into the canal at Medina. At Rochester a further supply is received from the Genesee Valley canal, with its Dansville branch, 124¾ miles in length. Two sources of supply thrown into the branch canal, the Oil creek reservoir and the Ishua creek, are 1,489 feet above tide-water.

Another reservoir exists at Rockville, and one of the forks of the Genesee is made available for it at Caneadea. A feeder is turned in at Wiscoy ; a feeder

at the Canese-raca creek, another at Allen's creek   The Genesee river is also
made subservient to the main canal at Rochester.   Whether this lateral supply
could be increased or not is not important, as all the requisite water thus far
can be obtained from Lake Erie.

The canal continues a further distance of 49 miles, entirely dependent on the
lockage supply, descending 118.5 feet, to 390.33 feet above tide-water, which
is the lowest level between Buffalo and the Rome reach, and accordingly, at the
eastern ascent from this level, the Lake Erie supply ceases.

The end of the reach, Port Byron, is situated 26 miles to the west of Syra-
cuse, where the junction with the Oswego branch takes place on a reach 10 feet
higher.   The distance from Buffalo is 158 miles.

The canal, having left the Lake Erie summit, has to depend for a water supply on what can be gathered.

Two summits succeed in the remaining 192 miles, which are taxed to feed,
beyond the Erie canal, the Seneca and Cayuga canal, and to a great extent the
Oswego and Oneida canals.

The length of the enlarged canal is 350..5 miles, with 71 locks, 7 feet deep,
110 feet long, by 18 feet wide.   The lockage is 654.8 feet.

The present locks admit boats 17 feet 6 inches wide, and 98 feet long, with 6
feet draught, carrying from 210 to 220 tons cargo.

The only improvement considered attainable is the construction of locks 220
feet long, and 26 feet wide, with the same depth of channel as at present, by
which means a superior class of vessels would navigate the canal.   The locks
themselves would exact much more than double the quantity of water supply
which is now demanded.   The vessels which at present pass by the Erie canal
can carry 7,000 bushels of wheat, 210 tons.   The enlargement would admit
vessels propelled by steam, carrying from 18,000 to 20,000 bushels of wheat.

We have in the above limit the maximum of enlargement hoped for, and it is
based on the admitted fact that increased depth cannot be attained.   If sufficient
water can be brought to the Rome reach to admit of large locks, and double the
present quantity would be indispensable for the same number of lockages, a
vessel drawing 6.3 feet, and entering the chamber of a lock 220 feet long, with
a width on the guards under 26 feet, is all that can be attained.

REVENUE OF THE CANADIAN CANALS.

Taking the revenue of the Chambly canal, in connection with the Saint
Ours lock, for they form one system of navigation, we find the return something
less than one per cent. on the cost, as is shown by deducting the charge of the
latter from the revenue of the former.

Chambly canal, net revenue, 1863	$9,183 36
St. Ours lock, excess of expenses	3,287 14
	5,896 22
The St. Anne's lock cost before the union	$19,860 02
Since the union	71,191 01
Total	91,051 03

Therefore, taken alone, it may be looked upon as paying something less than
4½ per cent. on the cost of its construction.   But it cannot be considered apart
from the Ottawa navigation, for it forms the eastern entrance to it.   It is possible that eventually the Ottawa canals may pay no small sum to the provincial

exchequer. But great improvements are called for in the Grenville and Carillon canals. At present they do not pay their expenses.

The St. Lawrence canals, in 1863, paid about three-fourths per cent; the Welland canal something over 2½ per cent., on the construction cost.

Of the total quantity of flour and grain sent eastward from the lake regions, the quantity sent via Montreal averages 11 per cent. in 9 years, while the receipts at Buffalo average 50 per cent. in 8 years.

There is no comparison between the two water routes from the lakes to the seaboard, one by the Erie canal to New York, the other by the St. Lawrence canals to Montreal. The advantage is entirely on the side of the St. Lawrence in every respect. The cost of transport, generally speaking, is about one-half. There is a difference of ten days' time in its favor, and it is estimated that the slowest means of transportation and the least cost is as rapid as the best on the Erie canal. The St. Lawrence vessels are of much greater capacity, and in every point of view the superiority is maintained. One would consider that with all these advantages the St. Lawrence would command not only the trade of western Canada, but also the commerce of the upper American lakes. On looking at the geography of this portion of the continent, the natural outlet for the whole territory certainly appears to be by the river, and it would be inferred that no other would be followed ; that by it supplies would be received, and exports transmitted, and that all effort to turn the commerce of the west from the river would be impossible. But the St. Lawrence is not followed ; and the vessels which bear the cargoes of cereals deposit them at the American lake ports for transfer to smaller craft, which descend the Erie canal. The Hudson is therefore the highway, and New York the port of the west.

There are many causes to explain this phenomenon, and it has been the long study of a few observing men to penetrate it. In divining the cause they discern the remedy. It is conceded that a ton of freight, in any form soever, arrives at Montreal from a given point in the west at half the cost of transport paid for its transfer to New York. On the other hand, freights from New York to Liverpool are always less than freights from Montreal to Liverpool ; as a whole, it results that it is more profitable to ship from New York. While the navigation is kept at the present limit, the relative cost will be maintained, and the system will be unchanged. The reason is evident. New York, from the imperfections of the St. Lawrence, is the importing market for the west, and consequently there are numerous vessels to bear away the produce delivered for export. In Montreal the number of vessels is limited. In the former case vessels seek for freights, and competition induces cheapness. In the latter, the freight seeks vessels, and high prices are maintained.

The present inequality of freight, so far as Canada is concerned, is established by the tables of trade. They show where one ton goes up, from four to five come down. Such is generally the case in agricultural countries. The exports exceed imports of equal value in bulk in the proportion of about four to one. As a consequence, there are not vessels to take the freights, or they must come not in ballast to do so ; and in either case, freights must rule high.

Vessels can profitably take the St. Lawrence only on condition that they can go through to the lake port, and then necessarily they would bring back what now goes by the Erie canal and the Hudson river to New York. The demands for freight on British vessels would be limited to Canada produce, much of which might possibly be carried by the sea-going propellers of Illinois and Michigan. From the limit at present imposed on sea-going vessels by the St. Lawrence above Montreal, no voyage above that port can be profitably made by the shippers. This fact must be borne in mind, as a result empirically determined. Accordingly, the western States seek the harbor of New York, not by choice, but by necessity. The importer of the lake States of the Union, did he desire to import by the St. Lawrence, would be understood by his neighbor who had brought in goods by New York. The treasury regulations of the United States operate entirely to the advantage of the Hudson, for the custom duties are calculated according to the goods' value at the country of manufacture. But at Montreal, owing to the necessity of transshipment, the duty would be levied on the value of goods there. No distinction of this character could be made if a western propeller could pass and return by the St. Lawrence. The impatience with which the western operator chafes under the restraint is well known.

The commerce of the northwest is not any fanciful speculation, nor is its magnitude in any way questionable. It is a reality, as inquiry will establish. It has outgrown the Erie canal, and the complaint of the west is that the quantity carried is so immense that carriers can command their own terms. The condition of the producers of the west has been described, without exaggeration, as that of men "shut out from the markets of the world, oppressed by the excessive production of their own toil, which remain wasting and worthless upon their hands, depriving labor of half its reward, discouraging industry, and paralyzing enterprise." Yet the prosperity of the west dates from the construction of the Erie canal. Indeed, the existence of these States may be traced to it, for no one of them can refer to more than forty years of settlement. It is the commerce of this region within that period which, more than any other influence, has raised New York to its present wealth. The form in which the contribution has been made, is what can generally be observed between the seaport and its dependencies. The imports for the west are delivered at New York. It is there that bulk is broken and the magazine of supply established. All cereals are delivered there for transfer to the east, or for shipment by the ocean; a tax is levied on every bushel of grain. Accordingly, every interest has received a stimulus, and a large city has grown up to be at the same time the London and the Paris of this continent. *The feeling, however, is strong that this profit has been derived at the expense of the west, and there is an unwillingness longer to submit to the exaction.*

There is only one mode by which these aspirations can be satisfied—by the creation of enlarged channels of communication. In many localities the produce is even without value, for it is without a market. It is estimated that 500 million bushels of Indian corn or maize are raised in the northwest; but not five per cent. of this amount finds its way to the seaboard, owing to the expense of getting it there; and that, out of the sixty cents paid in New England for a bushel of corn, only nine cents goes to the producer, the remainder being expended in freights and commission. *It is this sense of an inferiority of position which has hitherto led to great discontent in the west;* for, while Canada evinces its present indifference, New York will still control the carrying trade, and the Erie canal will defy competition. There is no necessity to nurse a commerce which has surprised the world by the constancy and rapidity of its increase, unless there be the possibility that it will seek other channels; and, although the Hudson offers the best route to the west, it is not the less unsatisfactory and exacting. We can, therefore, readily understand why, in the northwest, public attention has been turned to the Mississippi. There is a desire to improve the Illinois and Des Plaines rivers, and to enlarge the Illinois and Michigan canal to a navigation of locks 350 feet long, 75 feet wide, and seven feet deep, so that a more ample outlet may be obtained; and by turning to the Mississippi prevent the trade passing by the St. Lawrence, and accordingly retain it in the hands of the United States. Nevertheless, the increase of accommodation is peremptorily insisted upon. It has been argued that it is a national duty of the central government to extend it; that in reality the national exchequer could be no more than temporarily taxed; *that the import duties collected on the return cargoes purchased by the proceeds of exported food, now denied a market, would not only pay the interest of the cost of works, but would eventually pay the capital itself.* This surplusage of grain accounts for the extended pork trade. The hog is, indeed, regarded as corn in "a concentrated form." Maize is bulky and perishable, and it is found that it furnishes cheap food for animals. The latter, when killed and preserved, are in no danger of suffering from decay. They can be shipped at convenience. Accordingly, from four to five million hogs are annually slaughtered, varying from 200,000 to 250,000 tons.

There can be no ship canal from the west, except by the St. Lawrence. The advantages which it offers cannot otherwise be obtained. To make a ship canal to New York, even by Oswego, is an impossibility, and anything but a ship canal is of secondary importance to the west. The ocean is the prerogative of no State of the Union; and the west will seek the channel which conducts its commerce with the least cost and delay.

A full development of the navigation would at once change every consideration by which it is now regulated. Opposition from the Mississippi need not be argued, and there would remain only the Erie canal, which always must be limited and peculiar. This route retains its trade, not from being inherently preferable, but in spite of the disadvantage and the expense of navigating it, and the higher tolls it imposes. The advantages which it extends are to be found at its terminus.

The State of Illinois has officially represented the condition of the western States with great force. In 1863 the legislature passed a joint resolution appointing commissioners to proceed to Canada and solicit the earnest consideration and early action upon a subject of great and rapidly growing importance both to Canada and the west, "of enlarged and cheaper outlets to tide-water by way of the lakes and rivers, and new or enlarged canals of Canada."

This important document dwells upon "the growing and already vital necessity for enlarged and cheaper avenues to the Atlantic, and advances the importance, both to Great Britain and the United States, of so opening and perfecting the navigation of the St. Lawrence as to afford the commerce of both countries a cheap communication between the shipping ports on the northwestern lakes and Great Britain."

What the State of Illinois asks is a direct trade between the northwestern States and Liverpool, on the plea "that the increasing volume of business cannot be maintained without recourse to the natural outlet of the lakes." If this opportunity be vouchsafed, *and the requisite facilities be given, the surplus produce will be increased with a rapidity even beyond that of the past century.* It is estimated that from the State of Illinois alone there has been shipped annually, for the last ten years, a surplus of food sufficient to feed ten millions of people, and at the same time there has been a positive waste from the inability to bring the crops profitably to market.

The interior of North America is drained by the St. Lawrence, which furnishes for the country bordering upon the lakes a natural highway to the sea. Through its deep channel must pass the agricultural productions of the said lake region. The commercial spirit of the age forbids that international jealousy should interfere with great natural thoroughfares, and the governments of Great Britain and the United States will appreciate this spirit and cheerfully yield to its influence. The great avenue to the Atlantic through the St. Lawrence being once opened to its largest capacity, the laws of trade, which it has never been the policy of the federal government to obstruct, will carry the commerce of the northwest through it.

www.ingramcontent.com/pod-product-compliance
Lightning Source LLC
Chambersburg PA
CBHW021435090426
42739CB00009B/1490